ROYAL HISTORICAL SOCIETY
GUIDES AND HANDBOOKS

A

CENTENARY GUIDE

TO THE PUBLICATIONS OF THE

ROYAL HISTORICAL SOCIETY

1868–1968

AND OF THE FORMER

CAMDEN SOCIETY

1838–1897

BY

ALEXANDER TAYLOR MILNE

LONDON

OFFICES OF THE ROYAL HISTORICAL SOCIETY

UNIVERSITY COLLEGE LONDON, GOWER STREET, W.C.1

1968

© Royal Historical Society 1968

Made and Printed in Great Britain by Butler & Tanner Ltd., Frome and London

CONTENTS

INTRODUCTION

The object of this Guide is to provide a detailed list and index of all publications, apart from ephemeral notices and advertisements, issued by the Royal Historical Society since its foundation in 1868, and of those issued by the Camden Society, which was founded in 1838 and merged with the Royal Historical Society in 1897. The Camden Society was exclusively concerned with the editing of historical texts and after the merger of 1897 its publications were continued by the Camden series of the Royal Historical Society. As noted on pages 49–50 below the first volumes issued under the new arrangement were *Camden new series*, volumes 58–62, which bore the imprint of the Royal Historical Society, although prepared for the defunct Camden Society. With the *Third series*, the Camden series of the Royal Historical Society properly began. It has been used for the publishing of texts, usually with substantial introductions and editorial notes. A *Camden Miscellany*, in which two or more texts are printed in a single volume, has been issued from time to time, and altogether twenty-two of these *Miscellanies* have appeared within the four Camden series.

According to a brief account of the founding of the Royal Historical Society contained in its *Transactions* for the year 1878, the first meeting was held on 23 November 1868 and the first paper was given by Dean Hook. *Transactions of the Historical Society*, volume I, part 1, was issued in February 1871. The preliminary pages contained a list of contents (pp. 3–4), 'Laws of the Historical Society' (p. 5) and a 'List of Fellows' (pp. 6–8). Volume I, part 2, was issued early in the following year and it was apparently the intention to issue a third part, but before the end of the year the first two parts, which were continuously paged, were put together as a completed volume and issued with a new title-page: TRANSACTIONS OF THE HISTORICAL SOCIETY. EDITED BY THE REV. CHARLES ROGERS, LL.D., F.S.A.SCOT., HISTORIO-GRAPHER TO THE SOCIETY. VOL. I. LONDON: PRINTED FOR THE HISTORICAL SOCIETY. 1872. A new set of preliminaries (8 pages) included a 'Preface', by Charles Rogers (p. 3), a more summary list of contents (p. 5) and a revised list of Fellows (pp. 6–8). The rest of the volume occupied 530 pages and contained, according to Rogers, 'the Society's Transactions during its first two sessions, 1869–70 and 1870–71'. It did not, however, include Dean Hook's paper. In 1875,

Transactions of the Royal Historical Society, volume I, second edition, appeared. Although Rogers repeated in the Preface that this contained the Society's Transactions during 1869–70 and 1870–71, the two editions are not identical. The second edition was completely reset, with different pagination (448 pp., including the preliminaries). Two papers were omitted altogether, substantial alterations were made in two others and verbal changes in several more. Also omitted were two full-page plates which had embellished the first edition: *Sketch of supposed remains of two old Roman or British camps near Dunblane* (opposite p. 54) and *Monument of Sir Robert Aytoun in Westminster Abbey* (opposite p. 104). The quality of the communications to the Society during its early years was not high, but for those curious about the state of British historiography at the time attention may be called to a paper only to be found in the first edition of *Transactions*, volume I, pp. 249–78: 'The life of Fra Salimbene, 1221–1290', by T. L. Kington Oliphant; also to Sir John Bowring's paper on 'Latin aphorisms and proverbs' (pp. 82–103), which was considerably amended before it appeared in *Transactions*, volume II (1873), pp. 158–98, under the title 'Borrowings of modern from ancient poets'. That volume also contained a reprint of 'Notes on the history of Sir Jerome Alexander', by Charles Rogers, which had previously appeared in the first edition only of *Transactions*, volume I. Furthermore Rogers used his editorial discretion to change the title of his paper: 'Observations on the Scottish branch of the Norman house of Roger' and to widen its scope when he reprinted it in the second edition of volume I under the title 'The Scottish house of Roger, with notes respecting the families of Playfair and Haldane'.

Perhaps it was some misgiving about these changes which caused Charles Rogers to describe *Transactions*, volume II (1873) and volume III (1874) as 'Second series'. Although this misleading description was quickly dropped with volume IV, it has served to confuse many library catalogues. The first series was a short one and after ten volumes had been published a *new series* was started in 1884, probably because it had been decided to bring the *Transactions* out in quarterly parts, each part containing a new feature 'Bibliographical notices'. Unfortunately these notices of recent historical publications in Britain and abroad were as inadequate as the other work of the Society in those days, and the annual reports on 'The progress of historical research', which replaced them in 1891, were not much better. The quarterly issues were abandoned after 1886 and the progress reports ceased to appear after 1895. From time to time since a President or another Fellow has given information of the kind, but for the most part the *Transactions* have been confined to the printing of papers read to the Society.

With the 1901 volume of *Transactions*, the Society began listing its publications in an Appendix, but there was no indication of their contents until Hubert Hall produced in 1925 his brief *List and index of the publications of the Royal Historical Society, 1871–1924, and of the Camden Society, 1840–1897*. Still interesting for the notes they contain are the two editions of a *Descriptive catalogue of the works of the Camden Society*, compiled by John Gough Nichols. The first edition appeared in 1862, the second, which dealt with all the volumes in the 'Old series', in 1872. Quite useless is the over-ambitious *Catalogue of the first series of the works of the Camden Society, and Index* (1881). The compiler, Henry Gough, aimed at an exhaustive index of all persons, places and subjects mentioned in the volumes, but not surprisingly did not get beyond the entry 'Baudouin (John)' before his death. The fragment was published posthumously, with many blank pages for further entries appended, but no further sections were ever undertaken. Hall's *List and Index* errs in the opposite direction. It gives the titles of Camden texts and of papers in the *Transactions*, but without page references; while his two indexes of 'Authors, Editors and Titles' and 'Names, Places and Subjects' simply refer back to pages in the preceding lists.

The present *Centenary Guide* not only covers a longer period but gives much more detailed information. The contents of all publications of the two societies are fully listed, with exact page references. The General Index gives names of all authors and editors (indicating briefly under each the publications for which they were responsible), together with those of all persons, places or subjects mentioned either in the titles of papers and texts or in their analysed contents. To avoid a complicated system of numbers and letters, difficult to carry in the head, the various series are here listed continuously with easily recognised abbreviations. Thus the 265 volumes so far issued in the four *Camden series* are listed as C1 to C265, the 90 volumes of *Transactions* as T1 to T90, Miscellaneous Publications as M1 to M19 and so on. If, however, the key given at the beginning of the GENERAL INDEX (p. 147 below) is used, the reader need not turn back to the lists in the present volume to verify his reference, but may go direct to the volume concerned.

A. T. M.

CAMDEN SOCIETY

[OLD SERIES]

Volume I

C 1

Historie of the arrivall of Edward IV. in England and the finall recouerye of his kingdomes from Henry VI. A.D. M.CCCC.LXXI. *Ed.* John Bruce. Camden Soc., 1838. xv, 52, 12 pp.

> Pp. iii–xv, 1–40, Introduction; Text; 41–7, Notes; 49–52, Index; 1–3, note on the 'Camden Society for the publication of early historical and literary remains', lists of officers, including 'local secretaries'; 4–5, works published for 1838–9 and suggested for publication; 6–12, lists of members.

Volume II

C 2

Kynge Johan. A play in two parts. By John Bale. *Ed.* J. Payne Collier from the MS. of the author in the library of His Grace the Duke of Devonshire. Camden Soc., 1838. xv, 112 pp.

> Pp. v–xiv, Introduction; [xv], 'Persons in the two plays'; 1–103, texts of the plays; 105–10, notes; p. 112, Resolution of Council (16 July 1838), limiting membership of Society to 1000.

Volume III

C 3

Alliterative poem on the deposition of King Richard II. *Ricardi Maydiston De concordia inter Ric. II. et civitatem London. Ed.* Thomas Wright. Camden Soc., 1838. viii, 64 pp.

> Pp. v–viii, Preface; 1–51, texts of two poems, one in English, the other in Latin; 53–9, Notes; 60–4, Glossary.

Volume IV

C 4

Plumpton correspondence. A series of letters, chiefly domestick, written in the reigns of Edward IV, Richard III, Henry VII and Henry VIII. Edited by Thomas Stapleton from Sir Edward Plumpton's book of letters, with notices historical and bio-graphical of the family of Plumpton, com. Ebor. Camden Soc., 1839. [iii], cxxxix, 312 pp., folding Plumpton pedigree opp. p. ix.

> P. [i], Title page; [iii], Council of the Camden Society; pp. i–viii, Intro-duction; ix–cxxxviii, 'Historical and biographical notices of the family

of Plumpton'; 1–258, Letters written to Sir William Plompton (*temp.* Ed. IV), Sir Robert Plompton and others of family (*temp.* Hen. VII and Hen. VIII); 259–70, *Addenda et corrigenda*; 271–91, 'Index of matters'; 292–312, 'Index of places and persons'.

Volume V   C 5

Anecdotes and traditions, illustrative of early English history and literature, derived from MS. sources. *Ed.* William J. Thoms. Camden Soc., 1839. xxviii, 134 pp. [With inset pamphlet 'Facetiae of the seventeenth century' (12 pp.).]

Pp. vi–x, Preface; xi–xxviii, 'Notices of Sir Nicholas Lestrange and his family connections', communicated by J. G. Nichols; 1–79, 'Anecdotes and traditions', part 1, from Harleian MS. 6395, 'Merry passages and jests', by Sir Nicholas Lestrange (d. 1655); 80–116, part 2, from Lansdowne MS. 231, 'Remains of Gentilism and Judaism', by John Aubrey and White Kennett; 117–26, part 3, from Add. MSS. 3890, commonplace book of John Collet (*fl.* 1670); 127, 'L'envoy', by W. J. T.; 129–34, Index. [Bound with volume are Camden Society Report of Council, 1839; laws, list of members, etc. 32 pp.]

Volume VI   C 6

The political songs of England, from the reign of John to that of Edward II. Edited and translated by Thomas Wright. Camden Soc., 1839. xix, 408 pp.

Pp. vii–xvi, Preface; 1–345, transcripts, in Anglo-Norman, French, Latin and English, with introductory notes and footnotes; 347–402, 'Notes'; 403–8, Index.

Volume VII   C 7

Annals of the first four years of the reign of Queen Elizabeth, by Sir John Hayward, Knt. D.C.L. Edited from a MS. in the Harleian Collection by John Bruce. Camden Soc., 1840. l, 116 pp.

Pp. v–xl, Introduction; xli–xlvi, Will of Sir John Hayward; xlvii, certificate of his burial; xlviii–l, Catalogue of the works of Sir John Hayward; 1–107, transcript of his 'Annals'; 109–16, Index.

Volume VIII   C 8

Ecclesiastical documents, viz. I, A brief history of the bishoprick of Somerset from its foundation to the year 1174; II, Charters from the library of Dr. Cox Macro. Now first published by Joseph Hunter. Camden Soc., 1840. ix, 100 pp.

P. v, Advertisement; 3–7, Introduction to the history of the bishopric; 9–28, transcript of Latin text; 29–41, Notes; 45–8, Introduction to the charters and other Macro documents; 49–91, 11th–16th century transcripts, in Latin and English, with notes; 93–5, 'Index to the first portion'; 96–100, 'Index to the second portion'.

Volume IX   C 9

Speculi Britanniae pars: an historical and chorographical description of the county of Essex, by John Norden, 1594. Edited from the original manuscript in the marquess of Salisbury's library at Hatfield, by Sir Henry Ellis. Camden Soc., 1840. xliv, 42 pp., folding map.

Pp. ix–xliv, Introduction; 1–42, transcript. [Bound into volume: Camden Society, Report of Council, 1840, list of members, etc. (35 pp.)]

Volume X   C 10

A chronicle of the first thirteen years of the reign of King Edward the Fourth, by John Warkworth, D.D., master of St. Peter's College, Cambridge. Edited from the MS. now in the library of St. Peter's College, by James Orchard Halliwell. Camden Soc., 1839. xxvii, 79 pp., fac. opp. p. 1.

Pp. ix–xxvii, Introduction; 1–27, transcript of English text; 29–71, Notes; 73–9, Index.

Volume XI   C 11

Kemps nine daies wonder, performed in a daunce from London to Norwich. With an introduction and notes by Alexander Dyce. Camden Soc., 1840. xxvi, 35 pp., fac. of original title-page opp. p. 1.

Pp. v–xxvi, Introduction; 1–22, transcript of text of 1600 pamphlet; 23–35, Notes.

Volume XII   C 12

The Egerton papers. A collection of public and private documents, chiefly illustrative of the times of Elizabeth and James I, from the original manuscripts, the property of the Rt. Hon. Lord Francis Egerton, M.P., President of the Camden Society. *Ed.* J. Payne Collier. Camden Soc., 1840. viii, 509 pp.

Pp. v–viii, Introduction; 1–485, transcripts of MSS. with introductory notes; 487–91, 'Notes and corrections', 493–509, Index.

Volume XIII   C 13

Chronica Jocelini de Brakelonda, de rebus gestis Samsonis abbatis monasterii sancti Edmundi. Nunc primum typis mandata curante Johanne Gage Rokewode. Camden Soc., 1840. xi, 171 pp., illus.

Pp. v–xi, Preface; 1–103, transcript in Latin; 105–56, Notes; 157–9, Glossarium; 161–71, Index. [Frontispiece representing seal of Abbot Samson; facsimile of extracts from Harl. MS. 1005 opp. p. 1.]

Volume XIV   C 14

Narratives illustrative of the contests in Ireland in 1641 and 1690. *Ed.* Thomas C. Croker. Camden Soc., 1840. xv, 149 pp.

Pp. v–xiv, Introduction; 1–140, transcripts in English of 'The siege of Ballyally Castle in the county of Clare', by Maurice Cuffe (pp. 1–23), and '*Macariae excidium*, or the destruction of Cyprus, containing the last war and conquest of that Kingdom, written originally in Syriack by Philotas Phyloxypres, translated into Latin by Gratianus Ragallus P.R. and now made into English by C. O'K. [Charles O'Kelly], Anno Domini 1692' (pp. 24–107); 109–40, Notes and illustrations; 141–9, Index to both texts. [Bound into volume: Camden Society, pp. 3–10, Report of the Council, 1 May 1841; 10–12, Laws; 13–35, List of members.]

Volume XV   C 15

The chronicle of William de Rishanger of the Barons' Wars. The miracles of Simon de Montfort. Edited from manuscripts in the Cottonian Library by James Orchard Halliwell. Camden Soc., 1840. xlii, 162 pp., frontis.

Pp. v–xlii, Introduction; 1–65, transcript in Latin of *Chronicon Willelmi de Rishanger*; 67–110, transcript in Latin of *Miracula Simonis de Montfort*; 111–52, Notes and illustrations; 153–62, Index to both texts. Frontispiece shows facsimiles of Rishanger MSS.

Volume XVI   C 16

The Latin poems commonly attributed to Walter Mapes. Collected and edited by Thomas Wright. Camden Soc., 1841. xlix, [2], 371 pp.

Pp. v–xlv, Introduction, including 'Appendix (xxix–xlv) of pieces referred to in the Introduction'; xlvii–xlix, Contents; 1–267, transcript of Latin MSS.; 269–371, Appendix of translations and limitations, in Anglo-Norman, French, Latin and English (13th–15th centuries).

Volume XVII   C 17

The second book of the travels of Nicander Nucius, of Corcyra. Edited from the original Greek MS. in the Bodleian Library, with an English translation, by J. A. Cramer. Camden Soc., 1841. xxvii, 126 pp.

Pp. v–xxvii, Introduction; 1–95, transcript of MS. in Greek, with parallel English translation, describing visit to England *temp*. Henry VIII; 97–115, Notes; 117–26, Index.

Volume XVIII
C 18

Three early English metrical romances, with an introduction and glossary. Edited from a MS. in the possession of J. I. Blackburne, Esq., M.P., by John Robson. Camden Soc., 1842. xlv, 132 pp.

P. v, Council of the Society for 1841–2; vii–xxxvi, Introduction; xxxvii–xlv, Description of the manuscript; 1–93, transcript of manuscript in English, containing: 1–26, 'The anturs of Arther at the Tarnewathelan'; 27–56, 'Sir Amaduce'; 57–93, 'The avowynge of King Arther, Sir Gawan, Sir Kaye, and Sir Bawdewyn of Bretan'; 94–110, Notes; 111–30, Glossary; 131–2, *corrigenda* etc.

Volume XIX
C 19

The private diary of Dr. John Dee, and the catalogue of his library of manuscripts, from the original manuscripts in the Ashmolean Museum at Oxford, and Trinity College Library, Cambridge. *Ed*. James Orchard Halliwell. Camden Soc., 1842. viii, 102, 35 pp.

P. v, Council of the Society for 1841–2; vii–viii, Preface; 1–64, transcript of Diary; 65–89, *Catalogus librorum bibliothecae externae Mortlacensis D. Joh. Dee, Anno* 1583, *6 Sept*.; 91–102, Index to the Diary. [Bound into volume: Camden Society, pp. 1–10, report of General meeting, 2 May 1842, and Report of Council, 1 May 1842; 10–12, Laws; 13–35, Members.]

Volume XX
C 20

An apology for Lollard doctrines, attributed to Wicliffe, now first printed from a manuscript in the library of Trinity College, Dublin. With an introduction and notes by James Henthorn Todd. Camden Soc., 1842. lxiii, 207 pp.

Pp. v–lxiii, Introduction; 1–113, transcript in English; 115–88, Notes; 189–206, Glossary; 207, Errata.

Volume XXI
C 21

Rutland papers. Original documents illustrative of the courts and times of Henry VII and Henry VIII, selected from the private archives of His Grace the Duke of Rutland. *Ed*. William Jerdan. Camden Soc., 1842. xii, 133 pp.

Pp. vii–xii, Preface; 1–120, transcripts with introductory notes, viz. pp. 1–24, device for coronation of Henry VII; 25–7, livery allowed to

Sir Thomas Wriothesley at marriage of Louis XII and Mary (1514); 28–49, persons attending Henry VIII at Field of Cloth of Gold (1520); 49–58, device for meeting of Henry VIII and Charles V at Gravelines (1520), persons attending etc.; 59–100, hospitality etc. to Charles V during his visit to England (1522); 101–18, Household of Henry VIII; 118–20, claims to serve at coronation of Mary (1553); 121–5, Notes; 127–33, Index to volume.

Volume XXII   C 22

The diary of Dr. Thomas Cartwright, bishop of Chester; commencing at the time of his elevation to that see, August 1686, and terminating with the visitation of St. Mary Magdalene College, Oxford, October 1687. Now first printed from the original MS. in the possession of the Rev. Joseph Hunter. Camden Soc., 1843. xvii, 110 pp.

Pp. v–xvii, Preface; 1–93, transcript of diary, with footnotes; 95–110, Index of names.

Volume XXIII   C 23

Original letters of eminent literary men of the sixteenth, seventeenth and eighteenth centuries. With notes and illustrations by Sir Henry Ellis. C.S., 1843. vii, 460 pp., frontis.

Pp. v–vii, Preface; 1–451, transcripts, with notes, of correspondence of Nicholas Udall, Sir John Cheke, Roger Ascham, Laurence Nowell, John Dee, William Camden, Bodley, Speed, Ussher, Cotton, Strype, Sir Symonds D'Ewes, Ray, Sloane, Tillotson, Wanley, Prior, Hickes, Defoe, Tanner, Swift, Steele, Hearne, Benjamin Franklin, Sir Joseph Banks, the Abbé Mann and others; 453–60, Index.

Volume XXIV   C 24

A contemporary narrative of the proceedings against Dame Alice Kyteler, prosecuted for sorcery in 1324 by Richard de Ledrede, bishop of Ossory. *Ed.* Thomas Wright, C.S., 1843. [3], xlii, 64, 36 pp.

Pp. l–xxii, Introduction; xxiii–xlii, 'Appendix to the Introduction' [extracts in Latin concerning another trial for sorcery *temp*. Edward II and other writings about sorcery]; 1–40, transcript of Latin text; 41–58, Notes; 59–61, Additional note, with extracts on the same case from John Clynn's 'Annals'. [Bound into volume: Camden Society Report of Council, 1843, lists of members, etc. (36 pp.).]

Volume XXV   C 25

Promptorium parvulorum sive clericorum, lexicon anglo-latinus princeps, auctore fratre Galfrido Grammatico dicto e predicatoribus Lenne Episcopi, Northfolciensi, A.D. *c.* MCCCCXL, olim e prelis Pynsonianis editum, nunc ab integro, commentariolis subjectis, ad fidem codicum recensuit Albertus Way. Tomus I. 1843. xi, 319 pp., facsimile.

> Pp. v–xi, Advertisement; 1–318, transcript of MS. lexicon, letters A–L, with extensive notes; 319, Corrections. [Continued by vols. LIV and LXXXIX. The three volumes are often bound together.]

Volume XXVI   C 26

Three chapters of letters relating to the suppression of monasteries, edited from the originals in the British Museum by Thomas Wright. C.S., 1843. xvi, 304 pp.

> Pp. v–vi, Preface; vii–xvi, Contents; Three sections containing transcripts with notes as follows: 1–115, chapter I, 'The period previous to the passing of the act for the suppression of the smaller monasteries'; 116–252, chapter II, 'From the dissolution of the smaller houses to the passing of the act for the dissolution of the larger monasteries'; 253–92, chapter III, 'Final suppression of the monastic houses and confiscation of their property'; 293–304, Index [of names only].

Volume XXVII   C 27

Correspondence of Robert Dudley, Earl of Leycester, during his government of the Low Countries, in the years 1585 and 1586. *Ed.* John Bruce. C.S., 1844. [4], 1, 496 pp.

> Pp. i–xlvi, Introduction; xlvii–1, 'table of documents printed in this volume'; 1–457, Transcripts; 459–82, Appendix of illustrative papers, including, 461–6, 'A journal of My Lord of Leycesters proceading in the Lowe Countries, by Mr. Stephen Burrogh, Admiral of the Fleet'; 483–7, Notes and corrections; 489–96, Index.

Volume XXVIII   C 28

Croniques de London, depuis l'an 44 Hen. III. jusqu'à l'an 17 Edw. III. Edited, from a MS. in the Cottonian Library, by George James Aungier. Camden Society, 1844. [6], xxi, 112, 36 pp.

> Pp. i–xxi, Introduction; 1–93, text in Old French, with numerous notes; 95–103, Supplementary material; 105–12, Index. [Bound into volume: Camden Society, Annual General Meeting, Report of the Council, 1843–4, Report of auditors, Laws, list of members (36 pp.).]

Volume XXIX   C 29

Three books of Polydore Vergil's English history, comprising the reigns of Henry VI, Edward IV and Richard III, from an early translation preserved among the MSS. of the Old Royal Library in the British Museum. *Ed.* Sir Henry Ellis. C.S., 1844. [4], xxxix, 244 pp.

Pp. i–xxxii, Preface; xxxiii–ix, Appendix, containing transcripts of: two letters commending Vergil, a letter from Vergil to Erasmus and one from Erasmus to Vergil, a warrant for Vergil to leave the realm (1550) and Vergil's letter to Queen Mary I; 1–227, transcript of MS. translation into English; 228, List of errata; 229–44, Index.

Volume XXX   C 30

The Thornton romances. The early English metrical romances of Perceval, Isumbras, Eglamour and Degrevant; selected from manuscripts at Lincoln and Cambridge. *Ed.* James Orchard Halliwell. C.S., 1844. lvi, 312 pp.

Pp. v–xxiv, Introduction; xxv–1, Description of the Cambridge and Lincoln manuscripts; li–lvi, On the terminal contractions; 1–87, text of 'The romance of Sir Perceval of Galles'; 88–120, text of 'The romance of Sir Isumbras'; 121–76, text of 'The romance of Sir Eglamour of Artois'; 177–256, text of 'The romance of Sir Degrevant'; 257–306, Notes; 307–12, Glossarial notes.

Volume XXXI   C 31

Verney papers. Notes of proceedings in the Long Parliament, *temp.* Charles I, printed from original pencil memoranda taken in the House by Sir Ralph Verney, Knt. member for the borough of Aylesbury, and now in the possession of Sir Harry Verney, bart. *Ed.* John Bruce. C.S., 1845. xv, 191 pp.

Pp. v–xiii, Introduction; 1–182, transcript of MS. with introductory notes; 183–4, Appendix: I, undated MS. on 'Disbanding the armies'; II, 'Notes written in a cipher' [numbers, given 'in the hope that the ingenuity of some reader may discover their meaning']; 185–91, Index, Errata. [Bound into volume: Camden Society, Report of Council, 2 May, laws, list of members, etc. (36 pp.).]

Volume XXXII   C 32

The autobiography of Sir John Bramston, K.B., of Skreens, in the hundred of Chelmsford; now first printed from the original MS. in the possession of his lineal descendant, Thomas William Bramston, Esq., one of the knights of the shire for South Essex. [*Ed.* Lord Braybrooke.] C.S., 185, xx, 443 pp.

Pp. v–xvi, Preface; xvii–xx, 'Pedigree of Bramston'; 1–414, transcript of MS. autobiography (1611–1700), with preliminary account of family and especially his father, Sir John Bramston, the judge (1577–1654); 415–43, Index.

Volume XXXIII   C 33

Letters from James, Earl of Perth, Lord Chancellor of Scotland, etc., to his sister, the Countess of Erroll, and other members of his family. *Ed.* William Jerdan, C.S., 1845. xvi, 112 pp.

Pp. v–vi, Dedication to Lady Willoughby de Eresby; vii–xvi, Introduction; 1–108, transcripts of correspondence, 1688–96; 109–12, Index.

Volume XXXIV   C 34

De Antiquis Legibus Liber. Cronica maiorum et vicecomitum Londoniarum et quedam, que contingebant temporibus illis ab anno MCLXXVIII ad annum MCCLXXIV, cum appendice. Nunc primum typis mandata curante Thoma Stapleton. C.S., 1846. cclxxi, 276 pp.

Pp. i–ccxxxiv, Preface; ccxxxv, *Addenda*; ccxxxvi *Corrigenda*; ccxxxvii–cclxxi, Index to Preface; 1–177, transcript of Latin MS.; 179–253, Appendix containing additional material and notes; 255–6, *Errata et corrigenda*; 257–8, *Addenda*; 259–76, Index [to text].

Volume XXXV   C 35

The chronicle of Calais, in the reigns of Henry VII and Henry VIII, to the year 1540. Edited from MSS. in the British Museum by John Gough Nichols. C.S., 1846. xliii, 228 pp., illus.

Pp. xxvi–xlii, Preface; 1–48, transcript of chronicle in English; 49–213, Appendix of documents, with notes; 214, *Addenda et corrigenda*; 215–27, Index. View of Calais opp. p. xxvi, map, xxviii. [Bound into volume: Camden Society, Report of Council, 1845–6, list of members etc. 16 pp.).]

Volume XXXVI   C 36

Polydore Vergil's English history, from an early translation preserved among the MSS. of the old Royal Library in the British Museum. Vol. I, containing the first eight books, comprising the period prior to the Norman Conquest. *Ed.* Sir Henry Ellis. C.S., 1846. xv, 324 pp.

Pp. v–x, Preface; xi–xv, 'Appendix', containing two letters of Vergil and two of Henry VIII about him; 1–307, transcript of 'The cronicle of Polydore Virgil', books I–VIII; 309–24, Index.

Volume XXXVII   C 37

A relation, or rather a true account, of the island of England; with sundry particulars of the customs of these people, and of the royal revenues under King Henry the Seventh, about the year 1500. Translated from the Italian, with notes, by Charlotte Augusta Sneyd. C.S., 1847. xviii, 135 pp.

Pp. v–xviii, Preface, including (pp. vi–xviii) a list of Venetian ambassadors to England (1502–1763), prepared by John Holmes; 1–54, transcript in Italian with parallel English translation; 57–124, Notes; 125–31, Appendix giving text of inventory of 'apparell and wardrobe-stuffe' of Henry, Earl of Stafford, son of the Duke of Buckingham, 1528; 133–5, Index.

Volume XXXVIII — C 38

Documents relating to the foundation and antiquities of the collegiate church of Middleham, in the county of York; with an historical introduction and incidental notices of the castle town and neighbourhood. By William Atthill. C.S., 1847. xxix, 112 pp.

Pp. v–vi, Dedication to the Very Rev. P. S. Wood; vii–xxix, Preface; 1–60, Introduction, containing history of Middleham; 61–105, 'Documents' in Latin and English (c. 1478–1786); 106–110, *Addenda et corrigenda, Errata*; 111–12, Index.

Volume XXXIX — C 39

The Camden Miscellany, vol. I . . . C.S., 1847. Six items separately paged, viz.

(*a*) Register and chronicle of the abbey of Aberconway, from the Harleian MS. 3725. *Ed.* Sir Henry Ellis. C.S., 1847. 23 pp.

Pp. 2–4, Introductory note; 5–23, transcript of Latin text.

(*b*) Chronicle of the rebellion in Lincolnshire, 1470. *Ed.* John Gough Nichols. C.S., 1847. 28 pp.

Pp. 3–4, Introduction; 5–18, transcript of English text; 19–28, Notes.

(*c*) Bull of Pope Innocent VIII on the marriage of Henry VII with Elizabeth of York. Communicated by J. Payne Collier. C.S., 1847. 7 pp.

Pp. 3–4, Introduction; 5–7, reprint of English broadside version of the Bull (1485).

(*d*) Journal of the siege of Rouen, 1591. By Sir Thomas Coningsby, of Hampton Court, Co. Hereford. *Ed.* John Gough Nichols. C.S., 1847. 84 pp.

Pp. 3–12, Introduction; 13–65, transcript of English text; 66–81, Notes; 82–4, Index.

(*e*) Letter from George Fleetwood to his father, giving an account of the battle of Lutzen and the death of Gustavus

Adolphus. *Ed.* Sir Philip de Malpas Grey Egerton. C.S., 1847.
12 pp.

P. 3, Introduction; 4–12, transcript of English text, (22 Nov. 1622).

(*f*) Diary of Dr. Edward Lake, archdeacon and prebendary of
Exeter, chaplain and tutor to the princesses Mary and Anne,
daughters of the duke of York, afterwards James II, in the
years 1677–8. *Ed.* George Percy Elliott. C.S., 1847. 32 pp.

Pp. 3–4, Introduction; 5–31, transcript of English text; 31–2, Index.

Bound into volume: Camden Society Report of Council, 1846–
1847, list of members (16 pp.).

Volume XL C 40

A commentary of [*sic*] the services and charges of William Lord
Grey of Wilton, K.G., by his son Arthur Lord Grey of Wilton,
K.G., with a memoir of the author and illustrative documents.
Ed. Sir Philip de Malpas Grey Egerton. C.S., 1847. xxv, 83 pp.,
illus.

Pp. v–xxiv, Introduction; [xxv], explanatory note on map; 1–40, transcript of MS.; 41–80, Appendix of supplementary material; 81–3,
Index. [Frontispiece reproducing arms of Lord Grey of Wilton, 1557;
map of the castle and town of Guisnes between pp. xxiv and xxv.]

Volume XLI C 41

Diary of Walter Yonge, Esq., Justice of the Peace, and M.P. for
Honiton, written at Colyton and Axminster, Co. Devon, from
1604 to 1628. *Ed.* George Roberts. C.S., 1848. xxxii, 124 pp.

Pp. vii–xxxii, Introduction; 1–118, transcript of MS.; 119–24, Index.

Volume XLII C 42

The diary of Henry Machyn, citizen and merchant-taylor of
London, from A.D. 1550 to A.D. 1563. *Ed.* John Gough Nichols.
Camden Soc., 1848. xxxii, 464 pp., illus.

Pp. v–xiii, Preface; xiv–xix, 'Officers of state during the period of this
diary'; xx–xxxii, 'Note upon funerals' (engraving of funeral trophies of
Sir John White opp. p. xxxii); 1–312, transcript of Diary; 313–408,
Notes; 409–60, Index; 461–4, Glossarial index. [Bound into volume]:
Report of Council, 1848, list of members, etc. (19 pp.).]

Volume XLIII C 43

The visitation of the county of Huntingdon, under the authority
of William Camden, Clarenceux King of Arms, by his deputy

Nicholas Charles, Lancaster Herald, A.D. MDCXIII. *Ed.* Sir
Henry Ellis. Camden Soc., 1849. xv, 140 pp.

Pp. v–xv, Preface; 1–138, transcript of MS.; 139–40, Index.

Volume XLIV

C 44

The obituary of Richard Smyth, secondary of the Poultry
Compter, London; being a catalogue of all such persons as he
knew in their life; extending from A.D. 1627 to A.D. 1674. *Ed.* Sir
Henry Ellis. C.S., 1849. xxiii, 124 pp.

Pp. v–xxi, Preface; xxii, Pedigree of Richard Smyth; 1–105, text printed
from transcript in B.M. Sloane MS. 886 of lost original; 107–24, Index.

Volume XLV

C 45

Certaine considerations upon the government of England, by Sir
Robert Twysden, Knt. and Bart. Edited from the unpublished
manuscript by John Mitchell Kemble. C.S., 1849. lxxxv, 191 pp.

Pp. v–lxxxv, Introduction, including extracts from his journals; 1–181,
transcript of MS. written *c.* 1642; 182–91, Notes.

Volume XLVI

C 46

Letters of Queen Elizabeth and King James VI of Scotland,
some of them printed from originals in the possession of the
Rev. Edward Ryder, and others from a MS. which formerly
belonged to Sir Peter Thompson, Kt. *Ed.* John Bruce. C.S.,
1849. [4], xxii, [l], 180, 8 pp.

Pp. i–xxii, Introduction; 1–156, transcripts from originals formerly in
hands of Maitland family, or from copies in a volume entitled 'State
papers in the time of Queen Elizabeth and King James the 1st', once in
the Thompson Collection; 157–76, Appendix, containing further letters
from the Thompson Collection; 177–80, Index. [Bound into volume:
Camden Society Report of Council for 1848–9, etc. (8 pp.).]

Volume XLVII

C 47

Chronicon Petroburgense. Nunc primum typis mandatum
curante Thoma Stapleton. C.S., 1849. xv, 200 pp.

Pp. v–xv, Introduction by John Bruce (owing to death of the editor);
1–155, transcript of MS. 60, Society of Antiquaries of London; 157–83,
Appendix, transcript of *Liber Niger monasterii S. Petri de Burgo*; 185–
200, Index.

Volume XLVIII

C 48

The chronicle of Queen Jane, and of two years of Queen Mary,
and especially of the rebellion of Sir Thomas Wyat, written by

a resident in the Tower of London. Edited, with illustrative documents and notes, by John Gough Nichols. C.S., 1850. viii, 196 pp.

Pp. v–viii, Preface; 1–83, transcript of B.M. Harleian MS. 194, a diary (July 1553–October 1554), with introductory paragraphs from John Stow's *Annals* and footnotes; 84, 'Table shewing the heirs female in remainder to the Crown, named in the will of Henry VIII and the devise of Edward VI'; 85–179, Thirteen Appendices of relevant documents, including will of Edward VI, list of state papers of Queen Jane, texts of: *Epistle of Poor Pratte to Gilbert Potter* (pp. 115–21), John Elder's *Letter* on Philip II's arrival, triumphal processions and marriage to Queen Mary, and the legation of Cardinal Pole (pp. 134–66), list of state papers of Queen Mary, 1553–4; 180–8, Additions and corrections; 189–96, Index.

Volume XLIX   C 49

Wills and inventories from the registers of the commissary of Bury St. Edmund's and the archdeacon of Sudbury. *Ed.* Samuel Tymms. C.S., 1850. xii, 300, 8 pp., illus.

Pp. v–xii, Preface; 1–227, transcripts in Latin and English of MSS, 1370–1652; 229–67, Notes; 268, Index I—*Testatorum*; 269–77, Index II—*Nominum*; 278–82, Index III—*Locorum*; 282–300, Index IV—*Rerum*. [Bound into volume: Camden Society Report of Council, 1849–1850, list of members, etc. (8 pp.).]

Volume L   C 50

Gualteri Mapes De Nugis Curialium distinctiones quinque. Edited, from the unique manuscript in the Bodleian Library at Oxford, by Thomas Wright. C.S., 1850. xvi, 248 pp.

Pp. v–xvi, Introduction; 1–243, transcript of Latin text, with notes; 244, fragment by Map from Corpus Christi MS. 130, Cambridge; 245–8, Index.

Volume LI   C 51

The pylgrymage of Sir Richard Guylforde to the Holy Land, A.D. 1506, from a copy believed to be unique, from the press of Richard Pynson. *Ed.* Sir Henry Ellis. C.S., 1851. xvi, [2], 92 pp., illus.

Pp. v–xvi, Introduction; 1–85, reprint of text, with woodcut illustrations on pp. 1, 2, and 85; 87–92, Index.

Volume LII   C 52

Moneys received and paid for secret services of Charles II and James II, from 30th March 1679 to 25th December 1688.

Edited, from a MS. in the possession of William Selby Lowndes, Esq., by John Yonge Akerman, 1851. xi, [1], 240, 8 pp.

Pp. v–x, Preface; 1–213, transcript of MS.; 215–34, Index of persons; 235–38, Index of places; 239–40, Index of matters. [Bound into volume: Camden Society Report of Council, 1850–1, etc. (8 pp.).]

Volume LIII   C 53

Chronicle of the grey friars of London. *Ed.* John Gough Nichols. C.S., 1852. xxxvi, 108 pp., illus.

Pp. v–xxxv, Preface; xxxvi, reproduction of arms of Sir Richard Whittington, 1421; 1–98, transcript of English MS., covering years 1189–1556, with notes; 99–104, 'Additional notes'; 105–8, Index.

Volume LIV   C 54

Promptorium parvulorum sive clericorum, lexicon Anglo-Latinum princeps . . . Tomus alter. C.S., 1855. Pp. [i–iv], 319–439.

Volume II, transcript of items 'Macare'—'Rutton', with notes, in continuation of vol. XXV. [Bound into volume: Camden Society Report of Council, 1851–2, list of publications (10 pp.).]

Volume LV   C 55

The Camden Miscellany, vol. II . . . Camden Soc., 1853. Six items separately paged, viz.

(*a*) Account of the expenses of John of Brabant and Thomas and Henry of Lancaster, A.D. 1292–3. *Ed.* Joseph Burtt. Camden Soc., 1853. xvi, 18 pp.

Pp. iii–xvi, Introduction; 1–15, Latin transcript; 17–18, Notes.

(*b*) Household expenses of the Princess Elizabeth during her residence at Hatfield, October 1, 1551, to September 30, 1552. *Ed.* Viscount Strangford. Camden Soc., 1853. iv, 48 pp. illus.

Pp. iii–iv, Introduction; 1–48, transcript; two illus. opp. pp. 46 and 48.

(*c*) The request and suite of a true-hearted Englishman, written by William Cholmeley, Londyner, in the year 1553. Edited, from the original MS. in the library of the Faculty of Advocates of Edinburgh, by W. J. Thoms. Camden Soc., 1853. vi, 20 pp.

Pp. iii–vi, Introduction; 1–20, transcript of MS. advocating dyeing of wool in England.

(*d*) The discovery of the Jesuits' College at Clerkenwell in March 1627–8, and a letter found in their house (as asserted) directed to the Father Rector at Bruxelles. *Ed.* John Gough Nichols. Camden Soc., 1852. 64 pp.

> Pp. 1–20, Introduction; 21–62, transcript of MS. written by Sir Robert Heath, Attorney-General, with other material, and notes; 63–4, Index.

(*e*) Trelawny papers. *Ed.* William Durrant Cooper. Camden Soc., 1853. 23 pp.

> Pp. 3–5, Introduction; 7–23, transcripts of letters, etc. relating to Sir Jonathan Trelawny, bishop, and his father and grandfather (1644–1711).

(*f*) Autobiography and anecdotes, by William Taswell, D.D. sometime rector of Newington, Surrey, rector of Bermondsey, and previously student of Christ Church, Oxford, A.D. 1651–1682. *Ed.* George Percy Elliott. Camden Soc., 1852. 40 pp.

> P. 3, Introduction; 5–37, transcript; 39–40, Index.

Volume LVI   C 56

Letters and papers of the Verney family down to the end of the year 1639, printed from the original MSS. in the possession of Sir Harry Verney, bart. *Ed.* John Bruce. C.S., 1853. xvi, 308 pp.

> Pp. v–x, Introduction; xi–xiv, list of 'Letters and documents contained in this volume', folded sheet with pedigree of family opp. p. xiv, 1–276, letters and papers quoted with running commentary; 277–93, Appendix of financial documents; 295–308, Index.

Volume LVII   C 57

The Ancren Riwle; a treatise on the rules and duties of monastic life. Edited and translated, from a semi-Saxon MS. of the thirteenth century, by James Morton. C.S., 1853. xxviii, 480 pp.

> Pp. v–xxiv, Preface; xxv–xxviii, list of Contents; 1–431, transcript of MS. with parallel version in modern English; 433–79, Glossarial index 480, Corrections and additions. [Bound into volume: Camden Society Report of Council 1852–3, etc. (8 pp.).]

Volume LVIII   C 58

Letters of the Lady Brilliana Harley, wife of Sir Robert Harley, of Brampton Bryan, Knight of the Bath. With introduction and notes by Thomas Taylor Lewis. C.S., 1845. lii, 275 pp.

> Pp. v–xxxix, Introduction; xli–lii, Notes to Introduction; 1–209, transcripts of letters; 211–50, Appendix, mostly transcripts of other Harley correspondence of the period; 251–67, 'Notes to the letters'; 269–75, Index.

Volume LIX

A roll of the household expenses of Richard de Swinfield, bishop of Hereford, during part of the years 1289 and 1290. *Ed.* John Webb. C.S., 1853. xiii, 242 pp.

Pp. vii–xiii, Preface; 1–197, transcript of the roll and the endorsement; 201–42, Appendix of transcripts of relevant documents. [Work completed by Camden Old Series no. LXII].

Volume LX

Grants, etc., from the Crown during the reign of Edward the Fifth, from the original docket book, MS. Harl. 433, and two speeches for opening parliament by John Russell, bishop of Lincoln, lord chancellor. With an historical introduction by John Gough Nichols. C.S., 1854. lxviii, 96 pp.

Pp. v–xxxiv, 'Historical introduction'; xxxv–lxiii, transcripts, with introductory explanations, of the speeches in English; lxiv–lxvii, notes; 1–79, transcripts of grants, etc. in English or Latin; 81–3, Index I, 'Of offices and matters'; 84–6, Index II, 'Of places'; 87–94, Index III, 'Of persons'; 95–6, Index IV, 'Glossarial'. [Bound into volume: Camden Society, Report of Council, 1853–4, etc. (8 pp.).]

Volume LXI

The Camden Miscellany. Vol. III . . . C.S., 1855. Four items separately paged, viz.

(*a*) Papers relating to proceedings in the county of Kent, A.D. 1642–A.D. 1646. *Ed.* Richard Almack. C.S., 1854. vii, 68 pp.

Pp. iii–vii, Preface; 1–57, extracts from MSS. of Thomas Weller of Tonbridge; 58–61, Appendix of other Kent documents relating to the manor and castle of Tonbridge and to the Civil War; 63–8, Index.

(*b*) Ancient biographical poems on the duke of Norfolk, Viscount Hereford, the earl of Essex and Queen Elizabeth, from Gough's Norfolk MSS. in the Bodleian Library. *Ed.* J. Payne Collier. C.S., 1855. 26 pp.

Pp. 3–12, Introduction; 13–26, transcripts of MS. poems.

(*c*) A relation of some abuses which are committed against the Common-wealth; together with a freindlie reprehension of the same. Composed especiallie for the benefit of this countie of Durhame, December the 26th, 1629, by a poore freind & well-wisher to the Common-wealth. Edited from the original MS., preserved in the British Museum, by Sir Frederic Madden, C.S., 1854. iv, 35 pp.

Pp. iii–iv, Introduction, 1–27, transcript of MS.; 29–35, Notes.

(*d*) Inventories of the wardrobes, plate, chapel stuff, etc. of Henry Fitzroy, Duke of Richmond, and of the wardrobe stuff at Baynard's Castle of Katherine, Princess Dowager. Edited, with a memoir and letters of the duke of Richmond, by John Gough Nichols. C.S., 1855. c. 55 pp., illus.

Pp. iii–viii, Preface; ix–c, Biographical memoir of the duke, including correspondence and other documents, with additional notes (xc–c); 1–21, transcript of MS. inventory of the duke's wardrobe, etc.; 22–41, transcript of 'View of wardrobe stuff of Katharine of Arragon'; 42–8, 'Glossarial index'; 49–55, Index to the memoir.

Volume LXII   C 62

A roll of the household expenses of Richard de Swinfield, bishop of Hereford, during part of the years 1289 and 1290. Abstract, illustrations, glossary, and index. *Ed.* John Webb. C.S., 1855. Pp. [1–3], xiv–ccxxxii, 243–70, [1–8].

Pagination continued from vol. LIX. Pp. xiv–ccxxxii, 'Abstract and illustrations' in English; 243–9, Glossary; 251–67, 'General index' to both vols.; 269–70, *Addenda et corrigenda*. [Bound into volume: Camden Society Report for 1954–5, etc. (8 pp.).]

Volume LXIII   C 63

Charles I in 1646. Letters of King Charles the First to Queen Henrietta Maria. *Ed.* John Bruce. C.S., 1856. xxxi, 104 pp.

Pp. v–xxviii, Introduction; xxix–xxxi, Table of contents; 1–87, transcripts of letters, mostly from Charles (1645/6–1646/7); 89–101, Appendix, transcripts: five letters from Henrietta Maria to Charles, one from him to her, one from him to Montrose (1646–7); 103–4, Index.

Volume LXIV   C 64

An English chronicle of the reigns of Richard II, Henry IV, Henry V and Henry VI, written before the year 1471; with an appendix containing the 18th and 19th years of Richard II and the parliament at Bury St. Edmund's, 25th Henry VI, and supplementary additions from the Cotton MS. chronicle called 'Eulogium'. *Ed.* John Silvester Davies. C.S., 1856. xvi, 228 pp.

Pp. v–xvi, Preface; 1–110, transcript of English MS. of *Brute*; 111–18, 'An Appendix containing the 18th and 19th years of Richard II and the parliament at Bury St. Edmunds, 25th Henry VI, by Richard Fox.

monk of St. Albans' [extract from MS. in English]; 119–42, 'Supplementary additions from the continuation of the *Eulogium*, Cotton MS. Galba E. VII' [extracts in Latin]; 143–211, Notes; 213–28, Index.

Volume LXV C 65

The Knights Hospitallers in England; being the report of Prior Philip de Thame to the Grand Master Elyan de Villanova for A.D. 1338. *Ed.* Lambert B. Larking, with an historical introduction by John Mitchell Kemble. C.S., 1857. lxxii, 301 pp.

Pp. v–xi, Preface; xii–lxxii, Introduction; 1–214, transcript of MS. *Extenta terrarum et tenementorum Hospitalis Sancti Johannis Jerusalem in Anglia*; 215–20, Appendix, containing transcript of letter in Latin from preceptors and other members of Order in England to Master Elyan (July 1338); 221–45, Notes; 246, *Errata*; 247–300, Index; 301, *Addenda*. [Bound into volume: Camden Society Report for 1855–6, list of members, etc. (12 pp.).]

Volume LXVI C 66

Diary of John Rous, incumbent of Santon Downham, Suffolk, from 1625 to 1642. *Ed.* Mary Anne Everett Green. C.S., 1856. xii, 143 pp.

Pp. v–xii, Introduction; 1–131, transcript of MS. diary; 133–43, Index.

Volume LXVII C 67

Trevelyan papers prior to A.D. 1558. *Ed.* J. Payne Collier. C.S., 1857. ix, 219 pp.

Pp. v–vi, Preface; vii–ix, Contents; 1–219, transcripts in English and Latin, with footnotes. Chiefly drawn from the Trevelyan family muniments, but including documents from the public records, the Harleian collections and elsewhere. [Continued by vol. LXXXIV (See C 84).]

Volume LXVIII C 68

Journal of the Very Reverend Rowland Davies, LL.D., dean of Ross, and afterwards dean of Cork, from March 8, 1688–9, to September 29, 1690. Edited, with notes and an appendix, and some account of the author and his family, by Richard Caulfield. C.S., 1857. xv, 188 pp.

Pp. v–xii, Introduction; xiii–xiv, 'Pedigree of Davies of Richard's Castle' and related families; 1–156, transcript of MS. journal (with notes), describing visit to London, Great Yarmouth and other parts of England, return to Ireland and participation in the campaign against James II; 157–69, Appendix, extracts from Council-book of Cork corporation (Oct. 1690–9); 170–88, Index. [Bound into volume: Camden Society Report of Council, 1856–7. (8 pp.).]

Volume LXIX   C 69

The domesday of St. Paul's of the year 1222, or *Registrum de visitatione maneriorum per Robertum decanum*, and other original documents relating to the manors and churches belonging to the dean and chapter of St. Paul's, London in the twelfth and thirteenth centuries. With an introduction, notes and illustrations, by William Hale Hale. C.S., 1858. cxc, 211 pp.

Pp. vii–xvii, xix–lxi, Introduction; lxii–cxxxiv, Notes and illustrations; cxxxv–cxxxvii, Corrections and addition; 1–107, transcript in Latin of of the *Registrum*; 109–117, transcript from the Domesday of Ralph de Diceto, 1181; 118–75, other transcripts relating to manors belonging to St. Paul's; 177–211, Index.

Volume LXX   C 70

Liber famelicus of Sir James Whitelocke, a judge of the Court of King's Bench in the reigns of James I and Charles I, now first published from the original manuscript. *Ed.* John Bruce. C.S., 1858. [4], xx, 131 pp.

Pp. i–xx, Introduction; 1–111, transcript of MS., 1609–31; 113–18, Appendix, transcript from State Papers Domestic, 12 and 13 June 1613, of appearance of Sir Robert Mancell and Whitelocke before the Privy Council and admonishment; 119–31, Index. [Bound into volume: Camden Society Report of Council, 1857–8, etc. (8 pp.).]

Volume LXXI   C 71

Savile correspondence. Letters to and from Henry Savile, Esq., envoy at Paris, and vice-chamberlain to Charles II and James II, including letters from his brother, George, marquess of Halifax. Printed from a manuscript belonging to His Grace the Duke of Devonshire and from originals in Her Majesty's State Paper Office. *Ed.* William Durrant Cooper. C.S., 1858. [4], xxiv, 316 pp., pedigree.

Pp. i–xxiv, Introduction (inserted page containing Savile pedigree between pp. ii and iii); 1–303, transcripts of correspondence, with notes; 305–16, Index.

Volume LXXII   C 72

The romance of Blonde of Oxford and Jehan of Dammartin, by Philippe de Reimes, a *trouvère* of the thirteenth century. Edited, from the unique MS. in the Imperial Library in Paris, by M. Le Roux de Lincy. C.S., 1858. xxvii, 214 pp.

Pp. v–xxvii, Introduction; 1–214, transcript of MS. in Old French.

Volume LXXIII C 73

The Camden Miscellany. Vol. IV. C.S., 1859. Seven items, separately paged, viz.

(*a*) London chronicle during the reigns of Henry the Seventh and Henry the Eighth. Edited, from the original MS. in the Cottonian Library of the British Museum, by Clarence Hopper. C.S., 1859. iv, 21 pp.

Pp. iii–iv, Introduction; 1–18, transcript of MS. in English; 19–21, Index.

(*b*) The expenses of the judges of assize riding the Western and Oxford circuits, temp. Elizabeth, 1596–1601. Edited, from the MS. account book of Thomas Walmysley, one of the justices of the Common Pleas, by William Durrant Cooper. C.S., 1858. 60 pp.

Pp. 3–14, Introduction; 15–57, transcript of MS.; 58–60, Index.

(*c*) The Skryveners' Play, the incredulity of St. Thomas. From a manuscript in the possession of John Sykes, Esq., M.D., of Doncaster. *Ed.* J. Payne Collier. C.S., 1859. 18 pp.

Pp. 3–6, Introduction; 7–15, transcript of MS.; 16–18, Notes.

(*d*) The Childe of Bristow, a poem by John Lydgate. Edited from the original MS. in the British Museum, by Clarence Hopper. C.S., 1859. 28 pp.

Pp. 3–7, Introduction; 9–27, transcript of MS.; 28, Glossary.

(*e*) Sir Edward Lake's account of his interviews with Charles I on being created a baronet and receiving an augmentation to his arms. *Ed.* T. P. Langmead. C.S., 1858. 20 pp.

Pp. iii–xi, Introduction; 13–17, transcript of MS., 17–19, 'Copy of a Patent under the hand and seal of Sir William Dugdale, Norroy King of Arms, confirming the Armorial Augmentations to Sir Edward Lake; 20, Index.

(*f*) The letters of Pope to Atterbury when in the Tower of London. *Ed.* John Gough Nichols. C.S., 1859. 22 pp.

P. 3, Note; 4–20, extracts with comments; 21–22, Note.

(*g*) Supplementary note to 'The discovery of the Jesuits' College at Clerkenwell in March 1627–8, printed in the second volume of the Camden Miscellany [C56 (*d*) *above*], by John Gough Nichols. C.S., 1859. 10 pp.

Extracts and notes. [Bound in: Report of Council, 1858, etc. (8 pp.)].

Volume LXXIV   C 74

Diary of the marches of the royal army during the Great Civil
War, kept by Richard Symonds. Now first published from the
original MS. in the British Museum. *Ed.* Charles Edward Long.
C.S., 1859. xv, [2], 296 pp.

Pp. v–xiv, Introduction; xv, Corrections; two-page pedigree of Symonds
inserted between p. xv and p. 1; 1–280, transcript of MS. diary; 281–94,
Index of names and places; 295–6, Index of subjects.

Volume LXXV   C 75

Original papers illustrative of the life and writings of John
Milton, including sixteen letters of state written by him, now
first published from MSS. in the State Paper Office; with an appendix of documents relating to his connection with the Powell
family. Collected and edited, with the permission of the Master
of the Rolls, by W. Douglas Hamilton. C.S., 1859, viii, 140 pp.

Pp. v–vi, Preface; vii–viii, Contents; 1–74, transcripts of MSS. with
commentary; 75–134, Appendix of transcripts relating to Milton and
Powell families; 135–9, Index.

Volume LXXVI   C 76

Letters from George Lord Carew to Sir Thomas Roe, ambassador to the court of the Great Mogul, 1615–17. *Ed.* John
Maclean. C.S., 1860. xiv, 160 pp.

Pp. v–xiv, Preface; 1–139, transcripts, with footnotes; 140–6, Appendix
of explanatory notes; 147–60, Index.

Volume LXXVII   C 77

Narratives of the days of the Reformation, chiefly from the
manuscripts of John Foxe, the martyrologist; with two contemporary biographies of Archbishop Cranmer. *Ed.* John
Gough Nichols. C.S., 1859. xxviii, 366 pp.

Pp. v–x, Contents; xi–xxviii, Preface; 1–343, transcripts, with com-
mentaries, viz.: 1–59, 'The reminiscences of John Loude or Louthe,
archdeacon of Nottingham', with commentary; 60–8, 'The imprisonment of John Davis, a boy of Worcester, written by himself in after life';
69–70, 'Martyrdom of Edward Horne at Newent in 1558'; 71–84, 'Autobiographical narrative of Thomas Hancock, minister of Poole'; 85–131,
'The defence of Thomas Thackham, minister, in his conduct towards
Julins Palmer'; 132–76, 'Autobiographical anecdotes of Edward Under-
hill, one of the band of gentlemen pensioners'; 177–217, 'The troubles
of Thomas Mowntayne, rector of St. Michael Tower-Ryall, in the reign
of Queen Mary, written by himself'; 218–33, 'The life and death of

Archbishop Cranmer; 234–72, 'Anecdotes and character of Archbishop Cranmer', by Ralph Morice; 273–5, 'Cranmer and Canterbury school'; 276–8, 'The answers of Mr. Thomas Lawney'; 279–86, 'Chronicle of the years 1532–7, written by a monk of St. Augustine's, Canterbury'; 287–291, 'Summary of ecclesiastical events in 1554'; 292–351, Appendix of additional notes and documents; 353–6, Glossarial index; 357–66, General index.

Volume LXXVIII
C 78

Correspondence of King James VI of Scotland with Sir Robert Cecil and others in England, during the reign of Queen Elizabeth; with an appendix containing papers illustrative of transactions between King James and Robert, Earl of Essex. Principally published for the first time from manuscripts of the Most Hon. the Marquis of Salisbury, K.G., preserved at Hatfield. *Ed.* John Bruce. C.S., 1861. lv, 112 pp.

Pp. v–lv, Introduction; 1–76, transcripts of correspondence; 77–9, Appendix, Part I, Letters addressed to persons unknown; 80–110, Appendix, Part II, papers relating to Essex's conspiracy; 111–12, Index.

Volume LXXIX
C 79

Letters written by John Chamberlain during the reign of Queen Elizabeth. Edited from the originals by Sarah Williams. C.S., 1861. xiii, 188 pp.

Pp. v–xii, Introduction; xiii, 'pedigree of Sir Dudley Carleton, subsequently created Viscount Dorchester'; 1–180, transcripts of newsletters addressed to Carleton, 1597–1602; 181–8, Index. [Bound into volume: Camden Society, Report of Council, 1860–1 (4 pp.).]

Volume LXXX
C 80

Proceedings, principally in the county of Kent, in connection with the parliaments called in 1640, and especially with the Committee of Religion appointed in that year. Edited by Lambert B. Larking, from the collections of Sir Edward Dering, bart., 1627–44, with a preface by John Bruce. C.S., 1862. li, 253 pp., frontis.

Pp. v–li, Preface; 1–79, transcripts of correspondence, petitions, addresses and other electioneering documents; 80–100, 'Notes taken by Sir Edward Dering as chairman of the sub-committee of religion appointed Nov. 23, 1640'; 101–240, 'Petitions against the clergy from places in the county of Kent, with their answers and other papers relating thereto'; 241–53, Index. Frontispiece is reproduction of engraved portrait of Dering of 1644.

Volume LXXXI   C 81

Parliamentary debates in 1610. Edited, from the notes of a member of the House of Commons, by Samuel Rawson Gardiner. C.S., 1862. xx, 184 pp.

Pp. v–vii, Preface; ix–xx, Introduction; 1–146, transcript from British Museum Add. MS. 4210; 147–79, Appendix: transcripts of other MSS. relating to the Parliament: 147–52, Appendix A, report of Conference 26 April, 1610; 153–62, Appendix B, letter relating to King's reception of the House and enclosing Salisbury's speech, 28 July, 1610; 162–3, Appendix C, Bill against impositions; 163–79, Appendix D, imaginary conversation among Sir Julius Caesar's papers on ways and means, August, 1610; 181–3, Index; 184, *Errata.*

Volume LXXXII   C 82

Lists of foreign protestants and aliens resident in England, 1618–1688, from returns in the State Paper Office. *Ed.* William Durrant Cooper. C.S., 1862. [2], xxxii, 119 pp.

Pp. iii–xxxii, Introduction; 1–59, transcripts of lists among State Papers Domestic; 60–99, Appendix, transcript of 'A true certificat of the names of the straungers residing and dwellinge within the city of London . . .' (1618); 100–19, Index. [Bound into volume: Camden Society, Report of Council, 1861–2, list of members, etc. (4, 4 pp.).]

Volume LXXXIII   C 83

Wills from Doctors' Commons. A selection from the wills of eminent persons proved in the Prerogative Court of Canterbury, 1495–1695. *Ed.* John Gough Nichols and John Bruce. C.S., 1863. [4], viii, 175 pp.

Pp. i–vii, Introduction; [viii], list of wills in the volume; 1–161, transcripts of MS. wills and letters of administration; 163–7, 'Index locorum et rerum'; 167–74, 'Index nominum'; [175], 'Index testatorum, etc.'.

Volume LXXXIV   C 84

Trevelyan papers. Part II. A.D. 1446–1643. *Ed.* J. Payne Collier. C.S., 1863. viii, 139 pp.

Continued from vol. LXVII. Pp. v–vii, Contents; viii, 'Notice' about other Trevelyan MSS., including charters; 1–124, transcripts of MSS., with notes; 125–6, *Errata*; 127–36, Index of persons, parts I and II; 137–9, Index of places, parts I and II. [Bound into volume: Camden Society, Report of Council, 1862–3 (4 pp.).]

Volume LXXXV   C 85

The life of Marmaduke Rawdon of York, or Marmaduke Rawdon the second of that name. Now first printed from the original MS. in the possession of Robert Cooke, Esq. *Ed.* Robert Davies. C.S., 1863. xlii, 204 pp.

> Pp. v–ix, Contents; xi–xxxix, Introduction; xl–xlii, pedigree of Rawdon; 1–196, transcript of MS. biography, perhaps written by a kinsman of the same name, or by Marmaduke Harrison, a friend. The subject of the biography was engaged in Canary wine trade, early seventeenth century; 197–204, Index.

Volume LXXXVI — C 86

Letters of Queen Margaret of Anjou and Bishop Beckington and others, written in the reigns of Henry V and Henry VI, from a MS. found at Emral in Flintshire. *Ed.* Cecil Monro. C.S., 1863. xxi, 177 pp. + *errata* slip.

> Pp. v–xii, Table of contents; xiii–xxi, Preface; 1–167, transcripts of correspondence and other MSS.; 169–74, 'Index of names, etc.'; 174–5, Index of places; 176–7, 'Glossarial index'.

Volume LXXXVII — C 87

The Camden Miscellany. Vol. V. C.S., 1864. Six items, separately paged, viz.

(*a*) Five letters of King Charles II communicated to the Camden Miscellany by the Most Honourable the Marquis of Bristol, President of the Camden Society. C.S., 1864. 16 pp., illus.

> Pp. 3–5, Introductory note; 5–16, transcripts, with notes; frontispiece is facsimile page of holographs and royal seal.

(*b*) I, Letter of the Council to Sir Thomas Lake, relating to the proceedings of Sir Edward Coke at Oatlands; and, II, Documents relating to Sir Walter Raleigh's last voyage. Communicated by Samuel Rawson Gardiner, C.S., 1864. 13 pp.

> Pp. 3–6, transcript of Council's letter, [21 ?] July 1617; 7–13, transcripts from Proceedings of Privy Council, 1618.

(*c*) A catalogue of early English miscellanies, formerly in the Harleian Library. *Ed.* W. Carew Hazlitt. C.S., 1862. 34 pp.

> Pp. 3–6, Introduction; 7–34, text of catalogue.

(*d*) Letters selected from the collection of autographs in the possession of William Tite, Esq. . . . . C.S., 1864. 27 pp.

> Pp. 3–27, transcripts with comments and notes, of letters from Charles I, Oliver Cromwell, Admiral Robert Blake, George Monck (1st earl of Albemarle), Charles II (with appended list of commissioners to treat about the union of England and Scotland), and Nell Gwynn.

(*e*) Sir Francis Drake's memorable service done against the Spaniards in 1587, written by Robert Leng, gentleman, one of his co-adventurers and fellow-soldiers. Now first edited from the original MS. in the British Museum, together with an appendix of illustrative papers, by Clarence Hopper. C.S., 1863. 54 pp.

Pp. 3–8, Introduction; 9–23, transcript of MS.; 25–54, 'Appendix of letters and extracts from state papers connected with the expedition'.

(*f*) Inquiry into the genuineness of a letter dated February 3, 1613, and signed 'Mary Magdaline Davers'. C.S., 1864. 30 pp.

Transcript of letter describing court revels and notes identifying writer as Mrs. Magdalen Danvers (later Lady Danvers). [Bound into volume: Camden Society, Report of Council, 1863–4, etc. (8 pp.).]

Volume LXXXVIII C 88

Letters from Sir Robert Cecil to Sir George Carew. *Ed.* John Maclean. C.S., 1864. vii, 167 pp.

Pp. v–vii, Preface; 1–156, transcripts of MS. letters; 157–60, Appendix, 'Abstracts of letters not of sufficient interest to be printed *in extenso*'; 161–7, Index.

Volume LXXXIX C 89

Promptorium parvulorum. [Tomus III]. C.S., 1865. Pp. [1–4], xiii–lxxxvii, 439–563, [564–6], facsimile between pp. xl and xli.

Completion of work, of which parts I and II were issued as vols. XXV and LIV. The three parts are often bound into one or two volumes. Pp. xiii–xlix, Preface; l–lxxxv, Appendix: 'Notices of glossaries, vocabularies and other works illustrative of the English language and of medieval Latinity, and used, for the most part, in this edition of the *Promptorium*'; lxxxvi–lxxxvii, 'Index of the principal authors and works noticed in the Preface'; pp. 439–540, completion of transcripts from MSS.; 541–50, 'Orthographical index'; 551–9, 'Index of the principal subjects of the notes'; 560–3, 'Additional notes and corrections'; [566] instructions to the binder. [Bound into volume: Camden Society, Report of Council, 1864–5, etc. (8 pp.).]

Volume XC C 90

Letters and other documents illustrating the relations between England and Germany at the commencement of the Thirty Years' War [First series:] From the outbreak of the revolution in Bohemia to the election of the Emperor Ferdinand II. *Ed.* Samuel Rawson Gardiner. C.S., 1865. xl, 212 pp.

Pp. v–vi, Preface; vii–xxxv, Introduction; xxxvi–xl, Contents; 1–209, transcript of MS. letters and other documents in English, Latin, French and Spanish; 210–12, Index. [Continued by vol. XCVIII.]

Volume XCI   C 91

Registrum sive liber irrotularius et consuetudinarius prioratus beatae Mariae Wigorniensis. With an introduction, notes and illustrations, by William Hale Hale. C.S., 1865. xv, cxxviii, [366] pp.

> Pp. v–viii, Preface; ix–xv, list of Contents; i–xxxiv, Introduction; xxxv–cxxviii, 'Notes and illustrations to the Worcester register, A.D. 1240'; 1–8, transcript in Latin of 'contents of the flyleaves of the MS. written in a later hand'; 9a–174, Latin text of *Registrum* (the printed pages are numbered 9a, 9b and so on to 173a and 173b, to correspond to the two columns on each page of the original MS., completed about 1285); pp. 175–80 are transcripts of pages in Latin on the two final flyleaves of the original volume, in a hand of a later period; pp. 181–200, Index. [Bound into volume: Camden Society, list of works (2 pp.); Report of Council, 1864–5 (5 pp.).]

Volume XCII   C 92

Pope Alexander the Seventh and the college of cardinals, by John Bargrave, D.D., canon of Canterbury, 1662-1680. With a catalogue of Dr. Bargrave's museum. *Ed.* James Craigie Robertson. C.S., 1867. xxviii, 144 pp., frontis.

> Pp. v–vii, Contents; ix–xxviii, Introduction; 1–111, transcript of MS. with notes; 113–40, transcript of Bargrave's MS. catalogue; 141–4, Index.

Volume XCIII   C 93

Accounts and papers relating to Mary, Queen of Scots. *Ed.* Allan J. Crosby and John Bruce. C.S., 1867. [4], xxiii, 134 [136] pp., frontis.

> Pp. i–xxiii, Preface; 1–63, [part I, *ed.* A. J. Crosby], transcript of MS. accounts of expenses for Queen Mary's maintenance in England, funeral and burial; 63*–64*, Index; 65–134 [part II, *ed.* J. Bruce], transcript of anonymous MS. entitled 'A justificacion of Queen Elizabeth in relation to the affaire of Mary Queene of Scottes'. Frontispiece is folded two-page photolithograph reproduction of MS. showing 'The Standard, Great Banner, Helme and Crest, Coat of Arms, Sword and Targe, and Banner Rolles, at the Funerall of Mary Queen of Scotts'.

Volume XCIV   C 94

History from marble. Compiled in the reign of Charles II by Thomas Dingley, gent. Printed in photolithography by Vincent Brooks, from the original in the possession of Sir Thomas E.

Winnington, bart. With an introduction and descriptive table of contents by John Gough Nichols. C.S., 1867. [iv], 92, ccxl pp., illus.

> Pp. 1–21, Introduction; 21–44, 'Life and works of Thomas Dingley'; 45–46, Index to the Introduction; 47–92, 'Description contents of "History from marble" '; i–ccxl, facsimile reproduction by photolithography of first part of MS. recording and illustrating monumental inscriptions. [Continued by vol. XCVII. Bound into volume: Camden Society, Report of Council, 1866–7, etc. (8 pp.).]

Volume XCV   C 95

Manipulus vocabulorum. A dictionary of English and Latin words, arranged in the alphabetical order of the last syllables, by Peter Levins. First printed A.D. 1570; now re-edited, with a preface and alphabetical index, by Henry B. Wheatley. C.S., 1867. [5], xvi, 370 [255] pp.

> Note on preliminary page [5]: 'The present edition of Levins's *Manipulus vocabulorum* has been printed at the joint expense of the Early English Text Society, the Camden Society and the Philological Society.' Pp. i–xv, Preface; xvi, list of *errata*; 1–230, transcript of MSS., consisting of 8 pp. of Preface and 230 MS. pp., printed in double column and so numbered, but making 115 pp. in letterpress; 231–9, 'Notes and corrections of Latin words'; 240–368, 'Index of English words'; 369–70, 'Levins's original *errata*'.

Volume XCVI   C 96

Journal of a voyage into the Mediterranean, by Sir Kenelm Digby. A.D. 1628. Edited, from the original autograph manuscript in the possession of William Watkin E. Wynne, by John Bruce. C.S., 1868. xxxix, 106 pp.

> Pp. v–xxxviii, Preface; 1–95, transcript of MS.; 95–102, Additional notes; 103–6, Index.

Volume XCVII   C 97

History from marble . . . Volume the second. C.S., 1868. Pp. [i–iv], 93–196, ccxli–cccccxvii, illus.

> Facsimile edition concluded from Camden old series XCIV. Pp. 93–154, 'Descriptive table of contents' continued from previous volume; 155–72, Addenda; 173–80, Postscript; 180, list of *errata*; 181–96, Index; ccxli–cccccxvii, facsimile by photolithography of second part of original work. [Bound into volume: Camden Society, Report of Council, 1867–8, etc. (8 pp.).]

Volume XCVIII   C 98

Letters and other documents illustrating the relations between England and Germany at the commencement of the Thirty Years' War. Second series: From the election of the Emperor Ferdinand II to the close of the conferences at Mühlhausen. *Ed.* Samuel Rawson Gardiner. C.S., 1868. xi, 194 pp.

> Continuation of vol. XC. Pp. v–vi, Preface; vii–xi, Contents; 1–189, transcripts of letters and other MSS.; 190–2, Appendix, text of letter from Viscount Doncaster to the Marquis of Buckingham, 18/28 Aug. 1620; 193–4, Index.

Volume XCIX   C 99

Diary of John Manningham, of the Middle Temple, and of Bradbourne, Kent, barrister-at-law, 1602–3. Edited from the original manuscript by John Bruce, Esq., and presented to the Camden Society by William Tite, Esq. . . . 1868. [3], xx, 188 pp., frontispiece (fac.).

> Pp. i–xx, Preface; 1–172, transcript of MS. diary; 173–8, Appendix of documents on Manningham family; 179–80, *Addenda* and *corrigenda*; 181–8, Index.

Volume C   C 100

Notes of the treaty carried on at Ripon between King Charles I and the Covenanters of Scotland, A.D. 1640, taken by Sir John Borough, Garter King of Arms. Edited, from the original MS. in the possession of Lieutenant-Colonel Carew, by John Bruce. C.S. 1869. [4], xli, 82 pp.

> Pp. i–xli, Preface; 1–69, transcript of MS.; 70–82, Appendix, texts of relevant documents, including two broadsides. [Bound into volume: Camden Society, Report of Council, 1868–9, etc. (12 pp.).]

Volume CI   C 101

El hecho de los tratados del matrimonio pretendido por el principe de Gales con la serenissima infante de España Maria, tomado desde sus principios para maior demontración de la verdad, y ajustado con los papeles originales desde consta por el maestro F. Francisco de Jesus, predicador del rey nuestro señor. Narrative of the Spanish marriage treaty. Edited and translated by Samuel Rawson Gardiner. C.S., 1869. x, 350 pp.

> Pp. v–x, Preface; 1–102, transcript of Spanish text; 103–283, translation into English; 285–344, Appendix of relevant documents in English, Spanish and Latin; 345–9, Index; 350, *Errata*.

Volume CII

Churchwardens' accounts of the town of Ludlow, in Shropshire, from 1540 to the end of the reign of Queen Elizabeth. *Ed.* Thomas Wright. C.S., 1869. [4], vii, 184 pp.

Pp. iii–vii, 'Dedicatory preface' (addressed to Rev. Edward ff. Clayton, rector of Ludlow); 1–162, transcript of accounts (1540–74); 163–9, Appendix I, Extracts from the Churchwardens' accounts (1575–1600); 169–77, 'Remarks on the history of pews, as illustrated by the Ludlow Churchwardens' accounts, with extracts from the churchwardens' accounts of St. Michael Cornhill, in London'; 178, Appendix III, List of local and obsolete words found in the accounts; 179–82, Index; 182–4, Index of names.

Volume CIII

Notes of the debates in the House of Lords, officially taken by Henry Elsing, Clerk of the Parliaments, A.D. 1621. Edited, from the original MS. in the possession of Lieutenant-Colonel Carew, by Samuel Rawson Gardiner, C.S., 1870. ix, 158 pp.

Pp. v–ix, Preface; 1–127, Extracts from the Notes (omitting passages already printed in the *Lords' Journals*); 129–36, Appendix I, Proceedings in the House of Lords, 22–6 March 1621, from a minute-book in the Lords; 137–55, transcripts from other Lords' MSS.; 157–8, Index.

Volume CIV

The Camden Miscellany. Vol. VI. C.S., 1871. Three items, separately paged, viz.

(*a*) Life of Mr. William Whittingham, dean of Durham, from a MS. in Antony Wood's Collection, Bodleian Library, Oxford, with an Appendix of original documents from the Record Office. *Ed.* Mary Anne Everett Green. C.S., 1870. [2], ii, 48 pp.

Pp. i–ii, 'Notice'; 1–37, transcript of MS.; 38–40, note on widow, Mrs. Katherine Whittingham; 41–8, Appendices I and II, charges against Whittingham in Visitation of Durham.

(*b*) The Earl of Bristol's defence of his negotiations in Spain. Edited, from MSS. in the Bodleian Library and the Public Record Office, by Samuel Rawson Gardiner. C.S., 1871. [1], xxxix, 56 pp.

Pp. i–xxxix, Preface; 1–54, transcript of MS.; 55–6, Index.

(*c*) Journal of Sir Francis Walsingham, from December 1570 to April 1583. Edited, from the original MS. in the possession of

Lieutenant-Colonel Carew, by Charles Trice Martin. C.S., 1870. [1], ii, 104 pp.

Pp. i–ii, Preface; 1–99, transcript of MS.; 100–4, Index.

Volume CV C 105

Trevelyan papers. Part III, with introduction to parts I, II and III. *Ed.* Sir Walter Calverley Trevelyan, bart., and Sir Charles Edward Trevelyan. C.S., 1872, lix, 348 pp. *plus* five inserted pedigrees of Devon families, three of them folded-in.

Completed from vols. LXVII and LXXXIV. Pp. v–xlvii, Introduction to parts I, II and III; xlviii–lviii, Contents (of part III); lviii, Additional notes; 1–311, transcripts or extracts from MSS. dating from 1477 to 1776, chiefly letters of 17th century, with commentary and notes; 313–32, Appendix, Further transcripts mostly relating to activities of George Trevelyan in Civil War (1642–9); 333–6, Additional notes; 337, 'Additional notes and corrections to part I'; 337, list of 'Persons of the name of Trevelyan who have not yet been placed in the pedigree'; 338, *Errata*; 339–48, Index. Following page 348 is a folding pedigree of Trevelyan; then one of Willoughby (double page); then one of Steyning of Holnicott, Somerset (single page), with text on *verso* of tribute to Alice Frye, wife of Philip Steyning, on tablet in Washfield Church, Devon (1605); then pedigree of Culme (double page); and finally pedigree of Mallock, or Mallack of Axmouth, Devon (single page).

CAMDEN SOCIETY

NEW SERIES

Volume I   C 106

The Fortescue papers; consisting chiefly of letters relating to
state affairs, collected by John Packer, secretary to George
Villiers, Duke of Buckingham. Edited, from the original MSS.
in the possession of the Hon. G. M. Fortescue, by Samuel
Rawson Gardiner. C.S., 1871. [4], xxxv, 225 pp.

> Pp. i–xxv, Preface; xxvi–xxxv, Contents; xxxv, list of *errata*; 1–219,
> transcripts, chiefly of letters addressed to Buckingham or to Packer, on
> various matters (1607–44); 221–5, Index.

Volume II   C 107

Letters and papers of John Shillingford, mayor of Exeter,
1447–50. *Ed.* Stuart A. Moore. C.S., 1871. xxvii, 161 pp.

> Pp. v–xii, Contents; xiii–xxvi, Introduction; 1–132, transcripts of various
> letters and other documents relating to a suit brought against the mayor
> and citizens by Edmund Lacy, the bishop, and by the dean and chapter
> of Exeter; 133–54, Appendix, transcripts of other material relating to
> the dispute; 155–61, Index.

Volume III   C 108

The old cheque-book, or Book of remembrance, of the Chapel
Royal, from 1561 to 1744. Edited, from the original MS.
preserved among the muniments of the Chapel Royal, St.
James's Palace, by Edward F. Rimbault. C.S., 1872. [4], xx, 250
pp., illus.

> Pp. i–xix, Introduction; 1–180, transcript of MS.; 181–241, Notes; 241,
> list of *errata et corrigenda*; 243–8, Index of names; 249–50, Index of
> subjects and places.

Volume IV   C 109

A true relation of the life and death of the Right Reverend
Father in God, William Bedell, lord bishop of Kilmore in
Ireland. Edited, from a MS. in the Bodleian Library, Ox-
ford, and amplified with genealogical and historical chapters,

compiled from original sources, by the representative of the bishop's mother's family of Elliston, Thomas Wharton Jones. C.S., 1872. xvii, 268 pp.

Pp. vi–xi, Preface and dedication; xiii–xvii, Contents; xvii, list of *errata*; 1–82, transcript of MS. life; 83–252, 'Supplementary chapters, genealogical and historical'; 253–6, Appendix I, transcript of letter from Bedell to Sir Nathaniel Riche (9 Oct. 1627), describing his entrance to the duties of Provost of Trinity College, Dublin; 256–7, Appendix II, transcript of letter from Bedell to Sir Robert Bruce Cotton (10 Dec. 1627), concerning Ricemarch's Psalter; 258–9, Appendix III, Pedigree of the Bedell and Elliston families of Essex; 261–8, Index.

Volume V   C 110

The maire of Bristowe is kalendar, by Robert Ricart, town clerk of Bristol, 18 Edward IV. *Ed.* Lucy Toulmin Smith. C.S., 1872. [4], xvii, 129 pp., illus.

Pp. i–xxvi, Introduction; xvii, list of *errata*; 1–118, transcript of MS. mostly in English, with copious notes (The book is divided into six parts, the first three in chronicle form, the last three recording local laws and customs. Ricart's book, started in 1479, was continued by subsequent town clerks to the end of the 17th century); 119–29, Index. The three illustrations reproduced from the MS. are: (i) frontispiece, a photographic reproduction of the swearing-in of the mayor of Bristol, 1479; (ii) opp. p. xxvi, facsimile of Ricart's signature; (iii) opp. p. 10, a plan of Bristol, 1479. [Bound into volume: Camden Society, Report of Council for 1871–2 (4 pp.).]

Volume VI   C 111

Debates in the House of Commons in 1625. Edited from a MS. in the library of Sir Rainald Knightley, bart., by Samuel Rawson Gardiner. C.S., 1873. [4], xxiv, 190 pp.

Pp. i–xxiv, Preface; xxiv, *Errata*; 1–127, transcript of MS.; 128–51, Appendix I, 'Debates at Oxford' (another report of the 1625 Parliament, Harl. MSS. 5007 fo. 75); 152–63, Appendix II, 'Letters relating to the first Parliament of Charles I'; 164–78, Appendix III, 'Narrative of the course of public affairs in England', S.P. Dom. 1626; 179–86, Appendix IV, 'Mr. Pym's report on Mr. Montague's books, delivered in the second Parliament of Charles I'; 187–90, Index.

Volume VII   C 112

Military memoir of Colonel John Birch, sometime governor of Hereford in the civil war between Charles I and the parliament, written by Roe, his secretary. With an historical and critical commentary, notes and appendix by John Webb. *Ed.* T. W. Webb. C.S., 1873. [4], xv, 240 pp.

P. i, 'Preliminary notice' on editing of volume posthumously; iii–viii, Preface; ix–xiv, Historical introduction; 1–160, transcript of MS.; 161–199, notes; 201–36, Appendices of letters and other relevant documents; 237–40, Index. [Bound into volume: Camden Society, Lists of officers, Council, members, subscribing libraries (12 pp.).]

Volume VIII   C 113

Letters addressed from London to Sir Joseph Williamson while plenipotentiary at the congress of Cologne in the years 1673 and 1674. *Ed.* W. D. Christie. Volume I. C.S., 1874. [4], xvi, 198 pp., *errata* slip.

> Pp. i–xvi, Introduction; 1–198, transcripts. [Bound into volume: Camden Society, Report of Council, 1872–3 (5 pp.).]

Volume IX   C 114

Letters addressed from London to Sir Joseph Williamson. . . . Volume II. C.S., 1874. [4], 173 pp.

> Pp. 1–158, transcripts of letters continued from vol. VIII; 159–65, text of report by H. Ball to Williamson on 'The Paper Office, October 1674'; 167–73, Index to vol. II; 173, Index to Introduction (in vol. I).

Volume X   C 115

Account of the executors of Richard, bishop of London, 1303, and of the executors of Thomas, bishop of Exeter, 1310. Edited, from the original MSS. in the possession of the dean and chapter of S. Paul's, and from the archives of the city of Exeter, by the late venerable W. H. Hale and the Rev. H. T. Ellacombe. C.S., 1874. [6], xxx, 149 pp., illus.

> Pp. [5–6], Preface; i–xxix, Introduction; 1–45, transcript of MS. Compotus in Latin of Thomas Bitton, bishop of Exeter; 47–110, transcript of MS. compotus in Latin of Richard de Gravesend, bishop of London; 111–16, will of Richard de Gravesend, 1302; 117–38, Appendix I, Notes and observations; 139–43, Appendix II, 'Further notes about Clyst, the residence of Bishop Bitton, and the Chapel of S. Gabriel, spoken of in the Compotus'; 145–8, Index; 149, Index to the Introduction and Appendix. Illustrations: frontispiece, reproductions of Bishop Bitton's seal and a fragment of Bishop Gravesend's seal; opp. p. [6], pedigree of Bitton; opp. p. i, folding plate, showing chalice, paten and ring in Exeter Cathedral 'removed from Bishop Bitton's tomb in 1763'; opp. p. 1, seal of Matthew de Button, showing family arms; after p. 45, monumental slab, 'supposed to represent Robert de Botton' *or* Bitton. [Bound into volume: Camden Society, Report of Council, 1873–4 (5 pp.).]

Volume XI   C 116

A chronicle of England during the reigns of the Tudors, from

A.D. 1485 to 1559, by Charles Wriothesley, Windsor Herald. Edited, from a MS. in the possession of Lieutenant-General Lord Henry H. M. Percy, by William Douglas Hamilton. Vol. I. C.S., 1875. [4], xlviii, 226 pp.

Pp. i–xlviii, Introduction; 1–187, transcript of first part (1485–1542) of MS. in English; 189–226, Appendix, extracts, with notes, from King's Bench Baga de Secretis, pouches 8 and 9, Public Record Office, on the trials of Mark Smeaton, Henry Norreys, William Bryerton and Sir Francis Weston for adultery with Queen Anne Boleyn. [Continued by new series, vol. XX.]

Volume XII C 117

The quarrel between the earl of Manchester and Oliver Cromwell; an episode of the English Civil War. Unpublished documents relating thereto, collected by John Bruce, with fragments of a historical preface by Mr. Bruce, annotated and completed by David Masson. C.S., 1875. [4], xcviii, 102 pp.

Pp. i–ii, Introductory note; v–xcvii, 'Historical preface'; xcviii, '*Errata* in documents'; 1–58, correspondence of Manchester with the Committee of both Kingdoms (1644); 59–70, 'Narrative of the Earl of Manchester's campaign'; 71–7, 'Statement by an opponent of Cromwell'; 78–95, 'Cromwell's narrative. An accompt of the effect and substance of my narration made to this House [of Commons] for soe much thereof as concernd the Earle of Manchester'; 96–9, 'Notes of evidence against the Earl of Manchester'; 101–2, Index.

Volume XIII C 118

The autobiography of Anne Lady Halkett. *Ed.* John Gough Nichols. C.S., 1875. [4], xxiii, 118 pp.

Pp. i–xxi, Introduction; 1–107, annotated transcript of MS. covering years 1622–56, including much on royalist circles in England and Scotland during Civil Wars; 109–16, Appendix, 'Meditations' by Lady Halkett; 117–18, Index.

Volume XIV C 119

The Camden miscellany. Volume the seventh . . . C.S., 1875. Five items separately paged, viz.

(*a*) Two sermons preached by the boy-bishop at St. Paul's, *temp.* Henry VIII, and at Gloucester, *temp.* Mary. *Ed.* John Gough Nichols, with an introduction giving an account of the festival of the boy-bishop in England, by Edward F. Rimbault. C.S., 1875.

Pp. iii–iv, 'To the reader'; v–xxxvi, Introduction; 1–29, transcripts of the two sermons in English; 31–4, Appendix, text of 'Compotus

Nicholay de Newark', guardian of the property of John de Cave, boy-bishop at York, 1396.

(*b*) Speech of Sir Robert Heath, attorney-general, in the case of Alexander Leighton, in the Star Chamber, June 4, 1630. Edited, with a preface by the late John Bruce, by Samuel Rawson Gardiner. C.S., 1875.

Pp. iii–xiii, Preface, 'Leighton's case'; xiv–xxii, 'Note by the editor' (on Leighton); 1–10, Transcript of Heath's speech.

(*c*) Notes of the judgment delivered by Sir George Croke in the case of ship-money. Edited, from the MS. in the possession of the earl of Verulam, by Samuel Rawson Gardiner. C.S., 1875.

P. iii, Preface; 1–17, transcript of MS. notes in case of *Rex versus Hampden*, 1638.

(*d*) Letters relating to the mission of Sir Thomas Roe to Gustavus Adolphus, 1629–30. *Ed.* Samuel Rawson Gardiner. C.S., 1875.

P. iii, Preface; 1–84, transcripts of correspondence, with notes; 85–92, Appendix I, text of contemporary translation of 'Instructions of Gustavus Adolphus to Sir James Spens', 1624; Appendix II, 93–6, original Instructions in Latin; 97–8, Index.

(*e*) Receipts and expenses in the building of Bodmin church, A.D. 1469 to 1472. *Ed.* John James Wilkinson. C.S., 1874.

Pp. iii–vii, Preface; 1–49, transcript of accounts in Latin, or English.

Volume XV   C 120

Letters of Humphrey Prideaux, sometime dean of Norwich, to John Ellis, sometime Under-Secretary of State, 1674–1722. *Ed.* Edward Maunde Thompson. C.S., 1875. [4], xv, 221 pp.

Pp. i–xiii, Preface; xiv, *Corrigenda*; 1–207, transcripts of MS. letters, with notes; 209–21, Index. [Bound into volume: Camden Society, Report of Council, 1874–5 (5 pp.).]

Volume XVI   C 121

A common-place book of John Milton, and a Latin essay and Latin verses presumed to be by Milton. Edited, from the original MSS. in the possession of Sir Frederick U. Graham, bart., by Alfred J. Horwood. C.S., 1876. xx, 69 pp., illus.

Pp. v–xx, Introduction; 1–60, transcript of MS. commonplace book in Latin and English (folded-in facsimiles opposite pp. 23, 39 and 40);

61–3, 'Prolusion and verses [in Latin] presumed to be by John Milton';
64–6, 'List of authors cited by Milton in the commonplace book'; 67–9,
'References to some places in Milton's works where he has utilised entries
in the commonplace book'.

Volume XVII   C 122

The historical collections of a citizen of London in the fifteenth
century. Containing: I, John Page's poem on the siege of
Rouen; II, Lydgate's verses on the kings of England; III,
William Gregory's Chronicle of London. *Ed.* James Gairdner.
C.S., 1876. [4], lxii, 279 pp.

Pp. i–xli, Introduction; xlii–xlix, transcript of William Gregory's will
(1465) in English, with codicil in Latin (1466); 1–46, transcript of Page's
poem in English; 49–54, transcript of Lydgate's verses; 55–239, transcript
of Gregory's Chronicle covering 1189–1469; 241–58, Appendix, lists of
mayors and sheriffs of London (1199–1470); 258–62, 'Surrender of
Falaise Castle', text of articles; 263–4, Notes; 265–79, Index; 279, *Errata*.
[Bound into volume: Camden Society, Report of Council, 1875–6 (4 pp.).]

Volume XVIII   C 123

Documents relating to the proceedings against William Prynne
in 1634 and 1637. With a biographical fragment by the late John
Bruce. *Ed.* Samuel Rawson Gardiner. C.S., 1877. [4], xxxix,
121 pp.

Pp. i–xxxv, 'Biographical fragment by the late J. Bruce'; xxxvii–xxxviii,
Note by the editor; 1–100, transcripts of MSS., including Star Chamber
proceedings, petition of Prynne to Privy Council, sentence of the
University of Oxford on Prynne, correspondence, extracts from Privy
Council register and State Papers Domestic, newsletter from C. Ros-
singham, 15 June 1637, the will of Prynne; 101–18, Appendix, List of
Prynne's works by J. Bruce; 119–21, Index.

Volume XIX   C 124

Christ Church letters. A volume of mediaeval letters relating to
the affairs of the priory of Christ Church, Canterbury. *Ed.* J. B.
Sheppard. C.S., 1877. *vii*, xlvii, 113 pp.

Pp. *v–vii*, table of contents, i–xlvii, Introduction, 'Explanations and
illustrations'; 1–90, transcripts of 85 letters in Latin or English dated
1334–*c.* 1539; 91–108, Notes; 109–13, Index. [*Note:* C.S. new ser. vol.
XXI contains as frontispiece an illustration 'inadvertently omitted'
from this volume. [Bound into volume: Camden Society; lists of officers,
members and subscribing libraries (12 pp.), Report of Council, 1876–7
(5 pp.).]

Volume XX   C 125

A chronicle of England during the reigns of the Tudors, from
A.D. 1485 to 1559, by Charles Wriothesley, Windsor Herald.
Edited by William Douglas Hamilton. Vol. II. C.S., 1877. [iv],
170 pp.

> Pp. 1–146, continuation, from new series, vol. XI, of transcript for years
> 1547–59; 147–70, Index to vols. I and II.

Volume XXI   C 126

A treatise on the pretended divorce between Henry VIII and
Catharine of Aragon, by Nicholas Harpsfield, LL.D., archdeacon of Canterbury, now first printed from a collation of four
manuscripts, by Nicholas Pocock, C.S., 1878. [4], xi, 344 pp.,
frontis.

> Pp. i–ix, Preface; 1–302, text of treatise based on William Eyston's
> transcript of 1706 collated with three other copies (pp. 3–6 contain
> Eyston's explanatory letter to his son Charles, followed (pp. 7–11) by
> his note on 'The life and character of Doctor Harpsfield'; 305–37, Notes;
> 338–44, Index. The frontispiece contains facsimiles of the signatures of
> Cardinal Morton and Elizabeth of York, Queen of Henry VII 'in-
> advertently omitted from the volume of Christ Church Letters printed
> by the Camden Society' [new series, vol. XIX].

Volume XXII   C 127

Correspondence of the family of Hatton, being chiefly letters
addressed to Christopher, first Viscount Hatton, A.D. 1601–
1704. *Ed.* Edward Maunde Thompson. Vol. I. C.S., 1878. [4], ix,
243 pp.

> Pp. i–viii, Preface; ix, *Corrigenda*; 1–243, transcripts of correspondence,
> 1601–80, with footnotes. [Continued by vol. II, Camden new series, vol.
> XXIII. Bound into volume: Camden Society, Report of Council, 1877–8
> (3 pp.).]

Volume XXIII   C 128

Correspondence of the family of Hatton, being chiefly letters
addressed to Christopher, first Viscount Hatton, A.D. 1601–1704.
Ed. Edward Maunde Thompson. Vol. II. C.S., 1878. [iv], 275 pp.

> Pp. 1–251, transcripts of correspondence, 1681–1704, in continuation of
> new series vol. XXII, with footnotes; 253–75, Index to both volumes.

Volume XXIV   C 129

Notes of the debates in the House of Lords, officially taken by
Henry Elsing, Clerk of the Parliaments, A.D. 1624 and 1626.

by Henry B. Wheatley. C.S., 1882. lii, 432 pp., *errata* slip, and three unnumbered pages inserted between pp. xxvi and xxvii.

Pp. vii–xii, Preface; xiii–xxv, Introduction; [1–3], 'Note by the Director', with *corrigenda*; xxvii–lii, Additional notes; 1–428, text of wordbook; 429–32, 'List of principal authorities quoted from in the notes' . . . [Bound into volume: Camden Society, Report of the Council, 1881–2 (4 pp.).]

Volume XXXI   C 136

The Camden Miscellany. Volume the eighth . . . C.S., 1883. [4] pp. *plus* nine sections separately paged, viz.

(*a*) Four letters of Lord Wentworth, afterwards earl of Strafford, with a poem on his illness. *Ed*. Samuel Rawson Gardiner. C.S., 1883. iii, 9 pp.

P. [iii], Preface; 1–6, transcripts of letters addressed to earl of Carlisle, 1632–3; 7–8, poem of 1640, attributed to William Cartwright; p. 9, Index.

(*b*) Memoir by Madame de Motteville on the life of Henrietta Maria. *Ed*. M. G. Hanotaux. C.S., 1880. 31 pp.

Pp. 3–5, Note by the Director (S. R. Gardiner); 7–13, Introduction (in French); 17–18, Mémoire, Avertissement; 19–31, transcript of French MS.

(*c*) Papers relating to the delinquency of Lord Savill, 1642–6. *Ed*. James J. Cartwright. C.S., 1883. [1], ii, 33, ii pp.

Pp. i–ii, Introduction; 1–33, transcripts of correspondence, statements and other documents relating to Savill's forgery of a letter from English nobles to the Scots Commissioners inviting them to enter England; i–ii, Index.

(*d*) A secret negociation with Charles the First, 1643–4. Edited, from the Tanner MSS. in the Bodleian Library, by Bertha Meriton Gardiner. C.S., 1883. [l], xviii, 38 pp.

Pp. i–xviii, Preface; 1–37, transcripts of correspondence and other MSS. relating to Thomas Ogle's plan, with notes; p. 38, Index.

(*e*) A letter from the earl of Manchester to the House of Lords, giving an opinion on the conduct of Oliver Cromwell. *Ed*. Samuel Rawson Gardiner. C.S., 1883. [iii], 3 pp.

P. iii, Preface; 1–3, transcript of letter from Tanner MSS., [? Dec.] 1644.

(*f*) Letters addressed to the earl of Lauderdale. *Ed*. Osmund Airy. C.S., 1883. [1], ii, 44 pp.

Pp. i–ii, Preface; 1–43, transcripts of letters from Lord Cassilis, Lord Rutherford (later Lord Teviot), Lord Rothes, Lord George Douglas and Lord Holles; p. 44, Index.

(*g*) Original letters of the duke of Monmouth in the Bodleian Library. *Ed.* Sir George Duckett, bart. C.S., 1879. 13 pp.

Pp. 1–12, transcripts of two letters addressed to James II and one to the Queen, together with correspondence between T. Rawlinson and Samuel Jebb in 1743 about their discovery of them, with notes.

(*h*) Correspondence of the family of Haddock, 1657–1719. *Ed.* Edward Maunde Thompson. C.S., 1881. viii, 58 pp.

Pp. iii–viii, Preface; 1–55, letters from serving officers about naval operations; 57–8, Index; Haddock pedigree opp. p. viii.

(*i*) Letters of Richard Thompson to Henry Thompson of Escrick, Co. York. *Ed.* James J. Cartwright. C.S., 1883. [iii], 9 pp.

P. [iii], Preface; 1–8, transcripts of MS. letters, 1684–93 [?], including parliamentary news; p. 9, Index. [Bound into volume: Camden Society, Report of Council, 1882–3 (4 pp.).]

Volume XXXII

C 137

The voyage to Cadiz in 1625; being a journal written by John Glanville, Secretary to the Lord Admiral of the Fleet, Sir E. Cecil, afterwards Sir John Glanville, Speaker of the Parliament, etc., etc., never before printed, from Sir John Eliot's MSS. at Port Eliot. Edited, with introduction and notes, by Alexander B. Grosart. C.S., 1883. xlvi, 132 pp.

Pp. v–xxxi, Introduction; xxxiii–xlvi, Postscript, containing transcripts of two letters from Sir Edward Cecil to Sir John Coke, 8 Nov. 1625 and 27 Feb. 1625/6; 1–127, transcript of Glanville's MS.; 129–32, Index.

Volume XXXIII

C 138

Letter-book of Gabriel Harvey, A.D. 1573–80. Edited, from the original MS. Sloane 93 in the British Museum, by Edward John Long Scott. C.S., 1884. xix, 191 pp.

Pp. v–xvii, Preface; xviii, *Corrigenda*; 1–184, transcript of letter-book; 185–91, Index.

Volume XXXIV

C 139

The Lauderdale papers. *Ed.* Osmund Airy. Vol. I, 1639–67. C.S., 1884. [vi], 300 pp.

Pp. 1–283, transcripts and annotations of correspondence and other papers of John Maitland, 2nd Earl and 1st Duke of Lauderdale, with

Dublin by the way of the Isle of Man, 1750' [and back via Wales in 1751]. Later journeys are in C.S. new ser. vol. XLIV (1889). *See* C 149 *below*. [Bound into volume: Camden Society, Report of Council, 1886–7 (3 pp.).]

Volume XLIII C 148

Visitations of the diocese of Norwich, A.D. 1492–1532. *Ed.* A. Jessopp. C.S., 1888. lii, 335 pp.

Pp. vii–lii, Introduction; 1–319, transcripts in Latin of following visitations to religious houses: pp. 1–64, Bishop James Goldwell's (1492); 65–148, Bishop Richard Nicke's (1514); 149–95, Nicke's (1520); 196–261, Nicke's (1526); 262–319, Nicke's (1532); 320, list of religious houses visited; 321–35, Index nominum. [Bound into volume: Camden Society, Report of Council, 1887–8 (3 pp.); lists of officers, members and subscribing libraries (10 pp.).]

Volume XLIV C 149

The travels through England of Dr. Richard Pococke, successively bishop of Meath and of Ossory, during 1750, 1751, and later years. *Ed.* James Joel Cartwright. Vol. II. C.S., 1889. vi, 319 pp.

Continued from new ser. vol. XLII. Pp. v–vi, Preface; 1–294, transcripts from B.M. Addit. MSS. of his narrative of travels through England in 1754, 1756 and 1757; 295–319, Index.

Volume XLV C 150

Documents illustrating the impeachment of the duke of Buckingham in 1626. *Ed.* Samuel Rawson Gardiner. C.S., 1889. xiii, 305 pp.

Pp. v–xi, Introduction; xii, Contents; xiii, note of two *errata*; 1–302, transcripts as follows: 1–8, documents relating to the wardenship of the Cinque Ports; 9–17, neglect of guard of Narrow Seas; 18–70, seizure of French ship, St. Peter, of Havre-de-Grace; 71–138, extortions from East India Company; 139–302, loan of ships to the French; 303–5, Index.

Volume XLVI C 151

Memoirs relating to the Lord Torrington. *Ed.* John Knox Laughton. C.S., 1889. xii, 203 pp.

Pp. v–xii, Introduction; 1–175, transcript of account in B.M. Addit. MSS. 31958 of Admiral Sir George Byng's life to January 1705; 177–200, Appendix, some extracts from the MS. Journal of the Rev. Thomas Pocock, chaplain on the *Ranelagh* at the capture of Gibraltar, 1704; 201–203, Index. [Bound into volume: Camden Society, Report of Council, 1888–9 (3 pp.).]

Volume XLVII C 152

Essex papers. *Ed.* Osmund Airy. Vol. I, 1672–9. C.S., 1890. xii, 326 pp.

Pp. vii–xii, Preface; 1–324, transcripts from British Museum, Stowe MSS., for the period of Essex's vice-royalty of Ireland (222 items, including correspondence addressed to Essex from England and copies of his own letters, 1672–5); 325–6, Index. Supplemented by 3rd ser. vol. XXIV (1913). *See* C 191 *below*.

Volume XLVIII C 153

Visitations and memorials of Southwell Minster. *Ed.* Arthur Francis Leach. C.S., 1891. cxi, 234 pp., frontis.

P. viii, Note on seal of Southwell (reproduced as frontispiece); pp. ix–c, Introduction; ci–cviii, *Liber albus*, contents; cix–cxi, *Registrum capituli* (1469–1542), contents; 1–216, transcripts in Latin from the *Liber albus* and the *Registrum*, with marginal summaries in English and notes, of following texts: 1–95, Visitations and corrections (1469–1542); 96–145, wills proved before the chapter of Southwell (1470–1541); 145–89, admissions and resignations of canons, prebendaries, vicars choral, chantry priests, incense-burners and choristers; 190–6, copy of letter stating customs of York Minster (1106); 197–200, Southwell parish altar: ornaments, books and furniture (1369); 201–16, statutes of the Minster; 217–21, Index; 223–34, Index of names of persons. [Bound into volume: Camden Society, Report of Council, 1889–90 (3 pp.); lists of officers, members and subscribing libraries (10 pp.).]

Volume XLIX C 154

The Clarke papers. Selections from the papers of William Clarke, Secretary to the Council of the Army, 1647–9, and to General Monck and the commanders of the army in Scotland, 1651–60. *Ed.* C. H. Firth. Volume 1. C.S., 1891. lxxvi, 442 pp.

Pp. vii–lxxvi, Preface; 1–420, annotated transcripts from Worcester College MSS., chiefly correspondence, news-letters and debates of the Council of the Army in 1647; 421–9, Appendix A, introductory note and text of imprinted part of 'Colonel Wogan's narrative' concerning *The proceedings of the new-moulded Army* (1646–7); 430–3, Appendix B, 'The examination of the three troopers who delivered the letter of the soldiers to Major-General Skippon, April 30, 1647' (from Tanner MSS.); 434–5, Appendix C, A letter of Col. Richard Grevis to Sir Philip Stapleton, 30 May 1647; 435–9, Appendix D, A list of the Agitators elected in 1647; 440–2, Appendix E, Proceedings of the Council of the Army, 3–8 Nov. 1647. Continued by new ser. vols. LIV, LXI and LXII. *See* C 159, C 166, C 167 *below*. [Bound into volume: Camden Society, Report of Council, 1890–1 (3 pp.).]

Volume L   C 155

The Nicholas papers. . . . *Ed*. George F. Warner. Vol. II. January 1653–June 1655. C.S., 1892. xvii, 378 pp.

> Pp. v–xvii, Preface; 1–355, annotated transcripts of correspondence and other MSS., including many letters from Joseph Jane and others giving English news to Sir Edward Nicholas, while in the Low Countries and France; 357–78, Index. Continuation of new ser. vol. XL (1886); continued by new ser. LVII (1897) and 3rd ser. XXXI (1920). *See* C 145 *above* and C 162, C 198 *below*.

Volume LI   C 156

Accounts of the obedientiars of Abingdon Abbey. *Ed*. R. E. G. Kirk. C.S., 1892. lx, 196 pp.

> Pp. v–vi, Contents; vii–lvi, Introduction; lvii–lx, glossary; 1–142, transcripts in Latin, of accounts of officers of the abbey, the earliest 1322, the latest 1479, with headings and notes in English; 143–68, Appendix, summaries in English of bailiffs' accounts, court rolls and rentals of abbey lands (1384–1594); 169–95, Index; 196, List of *errata*. [Bound into volume: Camden Society: Report of Council, 1891–2 (3 pp.).]

Volume LII   C 157

Expeditions to Prussia and the Holy Land, made by Henry, Earl of Derby (afterwards King Henry IV), in the years 1390–1 and 1392–3; being the accounts kept by his treasurer during two years. Edited from the originals by Lucy Toulmin Smith, with introduction, notes and indices. C.S., 1894. [4], cxv, 360 pp.

> Pp. i–iii, Contents; v–viii, Prefatory note; ix–cxi, Introduction; cxiii–cxiv, List of *errata*; 1–292, annotated transcripts in Latin from wardrobe accounts of Richard of Kingston, archdeacon of Hereford, preceded by writs in Anglo-French appointing him treasurer for war and journeys (6 May 1390) and ordering audit of his accounts (1 Jan. 1391/2); 293–313, Notes; 315–26, Index I, Persons; 327–32, Index II, Places; 333–60, Index III, Glossarial. [Bound into volume: Camden Society, Report of Council, 1892–3 (3 pp.); Report of Council, 1893–4 (2 pp.); list of officers and list of publications, June 1893 (16 pp.).]

Volume LIII   C 158

The Camden Miscellany, volume the ninth . . . C.S., 1895. [4] pp. *plus* seven sections, separately paged, viz.

(*a*) Visitations of churches belonging to St. Paul's Cathedral, 1249–52. Edited from original manuscripts by W. Sparrow Simpson. C.S., 1895. xix, 38 pp.

Pp. iii–xix, Introduction; 1–33, transcript in Latin, with notes; 35–6, Index of names of persons and places; 37–8, Index of matters.

(*b*) 'The spousells' of the Princess Mary, daughter of Henry VII, to Charles, Prince of Castile, A.D. 1508. First printed by Pynson in two Editions, English and Latin. Edited from unique copies by James Gairdner. C.S., 1893. xvi, 38 pp., illus.

Pp. iii–xvi, Preface; 1–35, texts of Latin and English versions; 36–8, Index. Full-page reproduction opp. p. 1 of frontispiece in Latin edition, representing English royal arms supported by angels, with the Tudor rose and portcullis below.

(*c*) A collection of original letters from the bishops to the Privy Council, 1564, with returns of the justices of the peace and others within their respective dioceses, classified according to their religious convictions. *Ed.* Mary Bateson. C.S., 1893. vi, 84 pp., *erratum* slip.

Pp. iii–vi, Preface; 1–83, transcripts, with notes, of replies sent by the archbishops and bishops to questions in a letter from Privy Council, 17 Oct. 1564; p. 84, Index to dioceses.

(*d*) Papers relating to Thomas Wentworth, first earl of Strafford, from the MSS. of Dr. William Knowler. *Ed.* C. H. Firth. C.S., 1890. xii, 31 pp., *erratum* slip.

Pp. iii–xii, Preface; 1, list of papers; 2–31, copies of transcripts found among papers of Knowler, editor of Strafford correspondence (2 vols. 1739).

(*e*) Hamilton papers: Addenda. *Ed.* Samuel Rawson Gardiner. C.S., 1893. [iii], 42 pp.

P. iii, Preface; 1–39, transcripts of correspondence, 1647–8, with notes; 41–2, Index. Supplementing new ser. vol. XXVII. *See* C 132 *above.*

(*f*) Memoirs of Nathaniel, Lord Crewe. *Ed.* Andrew Clark. C.S., 1893. v, 48 pp.

Pp. iii–v, Preface; 1–46, transcript of biography, compiled from the Minutes of the Revd. Dr. John Smith, Prebendary of Durham (d. 1715), with additional material and notes; 47–8, Index.

(*g*) The journal of Major Richard Ferrier, M.P., while travelling in France in the year 1687, with a brief memoir of his life, compiled by Richard F. E. Ferrier and John A. H. Ferrier, two of his lineal descendants. C.S., 1984. 48 pp.

P. 2, Note on the date of the journey; pp. 2–14, memoir; 15–48, transcript of journal. [Bound into volume: Camden Society: list of officers, list of publications, June 1894 (16 pp.).]

Volume LIV

C 159

The Clarke papers. .... *Ed.* C. H. Firth. Vol. II. C.S., 1894. xxxix, 303 pp.

Pp. vii–xxxviii, Preface; including extracts from several letters giving biographical details about William Clarke and about the opposition to Cromwell; xxxix, *errata*, vols. I and II; 1–246, transcripts of correspondence and other Worcester College MSS. (1648–52); 247–53, Appendix A, Two Clarke letters from Leybourne Popham collection; 254–66, Appendix B, 'An account of the origin of the Agreement of the People and the negotiations of the officers of the army with the representatives of the Levellers, extracted from Lilburne's pamphlet, *The legal fundamental liberties*'; 267–8, Appendix C, A letter from Captain Anthony Mildmay, one of the attendants of the King, to his brother, Sir Henry Mildmay, 29 Feb. 1647/8; 270–82, Appendix D, List of officers attending at Councils and Committees, Nov. 1648–March 1649; 283–303, Index. [Bound into volume: Camden Society; list of officers and list of publications (16 pp.).]

Volume LV

C 160

Visitations of churches belonging to St. Paul's Cathedral in 1297 and in 1458. Edited from original manuscripts by W. Sparrow Simpson. C.S., 1895. lxx, 130 pp.

Pp. vii–viii, Preface; ix–lxx, Introduction, giving calendars and itineraries of the visitations and particulars of the parishes visited; 1–114, transcripts in Latin from archives of St. Paul's, with footnotes; 115–22, comparative 'Inventories of church goods taken 6 Edward VI in several of the parishes dealt with in the foregoing pages'; 123–6, 'Index of names of persons and places'; 127–30, 'Index of matters'. [Bound into volume: Camden Society; list of officers and publications, Feb. 1895 (16 pp.).]

Volume LVI

C 161

The archpriest controversy. Documents relating to the dissensions of the Roman Catholic clergy, 1597–1602. Edited from the Petyt MSS. of the Inner Temple, by Thomas Graves Law. Vol. I. Camden Society, 1896. xxviii, 248 pp.

Pp. vii–viii, Table of contents; ix–xxvii, Introduction; xxviii, List of *corrigenda*; 1–248, transcripts in English and Latin of correspondence and other MSS. (1597–1602). Continued by vol. LVIII. *See* C 163 *below.*

Volume LVII

C 162

The Nicholas papers. *Ed.* George F. Warner. Vol. III, July 1655–December 1656. Camden Society [and Royal Historical Society], 1897. xxii, 307 pp.

Continuing vol. L. Pp. v–xxi, Preface; xxii, *erratum* note; 1–292, annotated transcripts of correspondence and other MSS., including many from Joseph Jane, giving English news; 293–307, Index. Continued by 3rd ser. vol. XXXI (1920). *See* C 198 *below.*

Volume LVIII* C 163

The archpriest controversy. Edited for the Royal Historical Society by Thomas Graves Law. Vol. II Longmans, Green, 1898. xxxi, 262 pp.

Continuing vol. LVI. Pp. v–vii, Table of contents; ix–xxxi, Introduction; 1–248, transcripts of three groups of Petyt MSS., viz.: 1–44, 'Three English narratives', including John's Mush's Diary in Rome; 45–151, *Brevio relatio*, documents in Latin concerning negotiations of English Catholics in Rome and elsewhere (1587–1602); 152–248, 'Letters and memorials, 1601–1603'; 249–62, Index to both volumes.

Volume LIX* C 164

A narrative of the changes in the ministry, 1765–7, told by the duke of Newcastle in a series of letters to John White, M.P. *Ed.* Mary Bateson. Longmans, Green, 1898. xiv, 174 pp.

Pp. v–xiv, Preface; 1–169, transcripts from Newcastle Papers, British Museum, Add. MSS. 3303; 171–4, Index.

Volume LX* C 165

The narrative of General Venables, with an appendix of papers relating to the expedition to the West Indies and the conquest of Jamaica, 1654–5. *Ed.* C. H. Firth. Longmans, Green, 1900. xli, 180 pp.

Pp. v–xli, Preface; 1–105, transcript of copy among Edward Long Papers, B.M. Add. MS. 12429 ff. 7–72, collated with other versions; 107–115, Appendix A, copy of 'Oliver P. Instructions unto General Penn, Collonell Venables [etc.] for the manageing the southerne expedicion' (Stowe MSS. 185 f. 83), and their official commission (Add. MSS. 11410 f. 47), also Venables's instructions (Add. MS. 11410 f. 41); 116–22, Appendix B, contemporary lists of forces under Venables (1654); 123–6, Appendix C, Additional documents from Venables MSS.; 127–43, Appendix D, copies from Rawlinson MSS. of letters concerning the West Indian expedition (1655); 144–69, Appendix E, extracts from Henry Whistler's journal of the expedition (Sloane MSS. 3926); 170–3, Appendix F, Papers from Thurloe MSS.—a Spanish proclamation, letters from Cromwell to Monck and Lieut.-Col. Brayne (1556) on the expedition; 175–80, Index.

---

*Published for the Royal Historical Society following the amalgamation with the Camden Society on 2 May 1897.

Volume LXI* C 166

The Clarke papers. . . . *Ed.* C. H. Firth. Vol. III. Longmans, Green, 1899. xxviii, 217 pp.

Continued from new ser. vols. XLIX and LIV. Pp. v–xxviii, Preface; 1–196, transcripts from Worcester College MSS., including many extracts from newsletters, 1653–9, and correspondence; 197–202, Appendix A, 'Colonel Sexby's advice on foreign policy (Rawlinson MSS.); 203–8, Appendix B, 'Edward Montagu's notes on the debates in the Protector's Council concerning the last Indian [i.e. West Indian] expedition'; 209–17, Appendix C, 'An account of the fall of the Protector, Richard Cromwell, in a letter from Nehemiah Bourne' (Massachusetts Archives). Work concluded by vol. LXII. *See* C 167 *below.*

Volume LXII* C 167

The Clarke papers. . . . *Ed.* C. H. Firth. Vol. IV. Longmans, Green, 1901. xxiv, 331 pp.

Continued and concluded from new ser. vols. XLIX, LIV and LXI. Pp. v–xxiv, Preface; 1–270, transcripts from Worcester College MSS., 1659–60, including extracts from newsletters, correspondence, especially of General Monck, and other documents; 271–3, Appendix A, 'Certificates extracted from General Monck's order-book'; 274–6, Appendix B, 'Dr. Barrow's notes on the proceedings of General Monck'; 277–301, Appendix C, Letters selected from the Tanner and Carte MSS. (1659–1660); 302–3, Appendix D, The case of Sir Arthur Hesilrige; 304–6, Appendix E, Letter from Mr. G. Paul to King Charles II [1663], on Sir George Booth's rising and Sir Samuel Morland's joining the King's cause in 1659; 307–31, Index to vols III and IV.

---

* Published for the Royal Historical Society following the amalgamation with the Camden Society on 2 May 1897.

ROYAL HISTORICAL SOCIETY

Camden series

THIRD SERIES

Volume I   C 168

The Cely papers. Selections from the correspondence and
memoranda of the Cely family, merchants of the staple, A.D.
1475–88. *Ed.* Henry Elliot Malden. Longmans, Green, 1900.
liii, 214 pp., frontis.

> Pp. v–xlviii, Introduction; xlix–lii, Appendix I, 'Contemporary coinage';
> lii–liii, Appendix II, 'Contemporary wool marts'; 1–205, annotated
> transcripts from Cely MSS. in Public Record Office; 207–14, Index of
> names and places; 214, Index of letter-writers; frontispiece is facsimile
> of letter, 2 Sept. 1480.

Volume II   C 169

The despatches and correspondence of John, second earl of
Buckinghamshire, ambassador to the court of Catherine II of
Russia, 1762–5. Edited, with introduction and notes, by Adelaide
d'Arcy Collyer. Vol. I. Longmans, Green, 1900. ix, 256 pp.

> Pp. v–viii, Preface; ix, Table of contents; 3–69, Introduction; 73–238,
> extracts from Lord Buckinghamshire MSS. at Blickling, 1762–3; 241–54,
> Appendix, including text in French of the *Système politique* addressed
> by Bestouchef to the Czarina Elizabeth in 1744 or 1745 (pp. 241–53) and
> tables of imports and exports by the British factory at St. Petersburg,
> 1763 (pp. 255–6). Continued by vol. III. *See* C 170 *below*.

Volume III   C 170

The despatches and correspondence of John, second earl of
Buckinghamshire . . . *Ed.* A. d'Arcy Collyer. Vol. II. R.H.S.,
1902. x, 307 pp.

> Pp. v–x, Preface; 1–288, extracts from Blickling MSS., 1763–6; 291–2,
> Appendix, Note A, text in French of 'Article secret premier . . . et
> second' (of projected treaty between Britain and Russia, 1763); 293–5,
> Extract from ukase concerning Russian clergy, 1765; 297–307, Index
> to both volumes; 307, list of *errata*.

Volume IV   C 171

The Camden Miscellany. Volume the tenth . . . R.H.S., 1902. In three sections separately paged, viz.

(*a*) The journal of Sir Roger Wilbraham, Solicitor-General in Ireland and Master of Requests, for the years 1593–1616, together with notes in another hand for the years 1642–9. *Ed.* Harold Spencer Scott. R.H.S., 1902. xxi, 139 pp.

> Pp. v–xiii, Preface; xv–xxi, Table of contents (including summaries of portions of Journal not printed in volume); 1–117, extracts from Journal; 117–29, continuation (1641–9); 131–9, Index. [Chiefly concerned with English politics of period.]

(*b*) The travels and life of Sir Thomas Hoby, Kt., of Bisham Abbey, written by himself, 1547–64. *Ed.* Edgar Powell. R.H.S., 1902. xxiv, 144 pp., illus.

> Pp. v–xvi, Preface; xvii–xxii, Appendix to Preface, transcripts of documents relating to family and Bisham Abbey; xxiii–xxiv, Contents; 1–130, transcript of 'A booke of the travaile and lief of me Thomas Hoby' (visits to Germany, Italy and France etc.); 131–44, General index; folding pedigree of Hoby opp. p. xvi, facsimile of letter by Sir Thomas Hoby opp. p. 1.

(*c*) Prince Rupert at Lisbon. Edited for the Royal Historical Society by the late Samuel Rawson Gardiner. R.H.S., 1902. [v], 23 pp.

> P. iii, Preface; [v], Table of contents; 1–7, transcript, with notes, from B.M. Addit. MSS. 35251, of 'A brief relation of such passages and proceedings, as happened between the King of Portugall and his ministers on behalf of the King of Great Brittaine after the arrivall of His Majesty the King of Great Brittaine his fleet in the port of Lisboa' [Nov. 1649]; 8–21, Appendix, transcripts of muniments relevant to proposed treaty; 23, Index.

Volume V   C 172

The despatches of William Perwich, English agent in Paris, 1669–77, preserved in the Foreign State Papers of the Public Record Office, London. *Ed.* M. Beryl Curran. R.H.S., 1903. xx, 358 pp.

> Pp. v–xix, Preface; xx, note of *erratum*; 1–332, transcripts from P.R.O., State Papers, France, of letters mainly addressed to Sir Joseph Williamson and Lord Arlington; 333–58, Index.

Volume VI   C 173

Collectanea Anglo-Premonstratensia. Documents drawn from

the original register of the order, now in the Bodleian Library, Oxford, and the transcript of another register in the British Museum. Arranged and edited by Francis A. Gasquet. Vol. I. R.H.S., 1904. xxxvi, 264 pp.

> Pp. v–xxxvi, Preface; including (p. ix) a table showing houses of the order in England; 1–264, Part I, Generalia, Annotated extracts in Latin (except for an undated inventory in English, pp. 263–4), concerning relations between Prémontré and the English houses, elections of abbots, meetings of chapters, religious life, etc. Continued by vols. X and XII. *See* C 177, C 179 *below*.

Volume VII   C 174

Select despatches from the British Foreign Office archives relating to the formation of the Third Coalition against France, 1804–5. *Ed.* John Holland Rose. R.H.S., 1904. xii, 289 pp.

> Pp. v–xii, Introduction; 1–262, transcripts from Public Record Office, F.O. Russia and F.O. Prussia series:—part I (pp. 3–203), Russian despatches; part II (pp. 205–62) Lord Harrowby's mission to Berlin; 265–276, Appendix I, text of Anglo-Russian treaty of 11 April 1805, with the separate, secret and additional articles; 277–82, Appendix II, declarations of Count Stadion, Prince Czartoryski and Lord G. L. Gower, 9 Aug. 1805; 283, Appendix III, 'Stages of the progress of the First Russian Army'; 285–9, Index.

Volume VIII   C 175

The Presbyterian movement in the reign of Queen Elizabeth as illustrated by the minute book of the Dedham classis, 1582–9. Edited, from the MS. in the possession of J. F. Gurney, esquire, Keswick Hall, Norfolk, by Roland G. Usher. R.H.S., 1905. li, 105 pp.

> Pp. v–vi, Preface; vii, Contents; ix–li, Introduction, including, xxviii–xxix, 'The classes and their members' (lists); xxx–xxxiv, Bibliography; xxxv–li, 'a list of Puritan ministers concerned in the classical movement'; 3–21, annotated text of Richard Bancroft's hostile account entitled *Dangerous positions*; 25–74, annotated transcript of the Minute Book of the Dedham classis; 75–102, letters and papers illustrative of the Minute Book; 103–5, Index.

Volume IX   C 176

State trials of the reign of Edward the First, 1289–93. *Ed.* T. F. Tout and Hilda Johnstone. R.H.S., 1906. xlvi, 262 pp.

> Pp. v–vii, Preface (by Tout); ix–x, Contents; xi–xlv, Introduction; xlvi, Appendix to the Introduction, Additional cases (summarised); 1–92, annotated 'Select cases from roll 541 B', (Assize Rolls, Public Record

Office), in Latin; 93–9, Appendix I, transcript of the satirical *Narratio de passione justiciariorum*, with introductory note; 100–253, Appendix II, Analysis of roll 541 A; 255–62, Index.

Volume X   C 177

Collectanea Anglo-Premonstratensia. Vol. II. Arranged and edited by Francis A. Gasquet. R.H.S., 1906. xxviii, 267 pp.

Continuing C 173. Pp. v–xxvii, Preface; xxviii, list of *errata* in vol. I; 1–267, Part II, Specialia, annotated extracts in Latin, except inventory of Hales Owen, 1505 (pp. 263–5), relating to various houses of the order in England.

Volume XI   C 178

The acts and ordinances of the Eastland Company. Edited, from the original muniments of the gild of Merchant Adventurers of York, by Maud Sellers. R.H.S., 1906. lxxxviii, 175 pp.

Pp. vii–viii, Contents; ix–lxxxviii, Introduction; 1–69, transcripts of Acts and Ordinances of the Company (17th c.); 71–139, extracts from the Court Book of the York Eastland Company (1650–96); 141–66, Appendix: texts in Latin of Henry IV's charter to merchants trading with Norway (1408); Elizabeth I's charter to the Eastland merchants (1579); the proclamation in their favour of James I (1622), and its renewal by Charles I (1629), and other relevant documents; 167–71, Glossary; 173–5, Index.

Volume XII   C 179

Collectanea Anglo-Premonstratensia. Vol. III. Arranged and edited by Francis A. Gasquet. R.H.S. 1906. viii, 259 pp.

Continuing C 173, C 177. Pp. v–viii, Introduction; 1–224, Part II, Specialia, conclusion of annotated transcriptions in Latin under this heading, the houses arranged in alphabetical order from Langdon to West Dereham; 225–59, Index (to the three volumes).

Volume XIII   C 180

The Camden Miscellany. Volume the eleventh . . . R.H.S., 1907. [1], 210 pp. In four sections, continuously paged, viz.

(*a*) Some unpublished letters of Gilbert Burnett, the historian. Edited from an eighteenth-century transcript in the possession of Earl Spencer by Miss H. C. Foxcroft [corrected on title-page from 'Foxwell']. R.H.S., 1907.

Pp. 5–6, Prefatory note; 7–45, texts from transcript, with notes.

(*b*) Extracts from the papers of Thomas Woodcock, ob. 1695. Edited from the contemporary transcript by Dr. John Hall of Kipping, Thornton, near Bradford, Co. Yorks, by G.C.Moore Smith. R.H.S., 1907.

> Pp. 51–2, Prefatory note; 53–89, text from the Hall transcript, with notes.

(*c*) The memoirs of Sir George Courthop, 1616–85. Edited, from an eighteenth-century transcript in the possession of G. J. Courthope, esquire, by Mrs. S. C. Lomas. R.H.S., 1907.

> Pp. 95–100, Preface; 101, Preface by the transcriber, Edmund Ferrers, 1801; text of transcription, 103–54; 155–7, Appendix, by Ferrers, giving monumental inscriptions about Sir George and his family.

(*d*) The Commonwealth charter of the city of Salisbury, [12] September 1656. Edited, from the contemporary copy of the original charter in the possession of the mayor and corporation and the enrolment in the Court of Exchequer, by Hubert Hall. R.H.S., 1907.

> Pp. 163–6, Preface; 167–98, transcript collated with enrolment; 199–210, Index (to the whole volume).

Volume XIV   C 181

The relation of Sydnam Poyntz, 1624–36. *Ed.* A. T. S. Goodrick. R.H.S., 1908. [vii], 155 pp., *erratum* slip.

> P. vi, *Erratum* and *addendum*; 1–44, Introduction; 45–137, Autobiographical narrative of Thirty Years' War transcribed from MS. in Bibliothèque Nationale, Paris: 'A true relation of these German warres from Mansfield's going out of England which was in the yeare 1624 until this last year 1636, whereof my self was an eywitnesse of most I have here related as followeth'; 139–44, Appendix A, 'The replication of William Poyntz gentt complaynant to the answer of Katherine Golder, widowe defendant' (attempt by brother after death of Sydnam to recover £50 apprenticeship premium); 145, Appendix B, extract from *The vindication of Colonel General Poyntz against . . . slanders* (1645); 146–7, Appendix C, note on diary of Fritzch, a German soldier, covering same period; 149–55, Index.

Volume XV   C 182

The diary of the Rev. Ralph Josselin, 1616–83. *Ed.* E. Hockliffe. R.H.S., 1908. xi, 192 pp.

> Pp. v–ix, Preface; 1–183, extracts from diary of Puritan vicar of Earls Colne (1640–83); 185–92, Index.

Volume XVI C 183

Despatches from Paris, 1784–90. Selected and edited from the Foreign Office correspondence by Oscar Browning. Vol. I, 1784–7. R.H.S., 1909. xi, 278 pp.

P. v, Prefatory note; vii–xi, List of *errata*; 1–278, transcripts of despatches from duke of Dorset and other British ministers in Paris from P.R.O., F.O. France series. Continued by 3rd ser. vol. XIX (1910). *See* C 186 *below.*

Volume XVII C 184

The Bardon papers. Documents relating to the imprisonment and trial of Mary, Queen of Scots. *Ed.* Conyers Read, with a prefatory note by Charles Cotton. R.H.S., 1909. xlvii, 139 pp.

Pp. vii–viii, Contents; ix–xi, Preface; xiii–xlv, Introduction; 1–109, transcripts from British Museum, Egerton MSS. 2124, of papers formerly at Bardon House, Somerset, perhaps collected by Sir Christopher Hatton; 113–27, Appendix I, Petition presented to Elizabeth by Parliament, May 1572, urging her to debar Mary Stuart from the succession to the English crown (from B.M. Cotton MSS.); 128, Appendix II, Secretary Walsingham's notes upon certain offers made by Mary Stuart, 21 April 1583 (from P.R.O. State Papers, Mary, Queen of Scots); 129–33, Appendix III, commentary on Mary Stuart's letter to Babington, 17 July 1586; 134–9, Index.

Volume XVIII C 185

Camden Miscellany, Vol. XII. R.H.S., 1910. x, 301 pp. In four sections continuously paged, viz.

(*a*) Two London chronicles from the collections of John Stow. *Ed.* Charles Lethbridge Kingsford. R.H.S., 1910.

Pp. v–x, Introduction; 1–43, transcript of 'A London chronicle, 1523–1555'; 44–9, transcript of 'A brief London chronicle, 1547–64'; 51–7, Index (to both chronicles).

(*b*) Life of Sir John Digby, 1605–45, now first printed from the MS. in the Bibliothèque Nationale, Paris. *Ed.* Georges Bernard. R.H.S., 1910.

Pp. 63–5, Preface; 67–119, text of life, probably by Edward Walsingham; 121–46, Poems written in honour of Sir John Digby, Sir John Smith, Sir John Gage and others; 147–9, Index.

(*c*) *Iter bellicosum.* Adam Wheeler his account of 1685. *Ed.* Henry Elliot Malden. R.H.S., 1910.

P. 154, Plan showing movement of troops before battle of Sedgemoor (1685); pp. 155–8, Preface; 159–66, transcript of MS. account of march of Col. John Windham's regiment of foot to battle and the actual engagement; 167–8, Index.

(*d*) Common rights at Cottenham and Stretham in Cambridgeshire. *Ed*. W. Cunningham. R.H.S., 1910.

Pp. 173–91, Preface; 193–289, copies of earlier transcripts of MS. agreements, orders and bye-laws, 16th and 17th centuries; 291–6, Index.

Volume XIX   C 186

Despatches from Paris, 1784–90. Selected and edited from the Foreign Office correspondence by Oscar Browning. Vol. II, 1788–90. R.H.S., 1910. x, 337 pp.

Pp. vii–x, Preface; 3–329, transcripts of despatches from Lord Dorset, Lord Fitzgerald and others from P.R.O., F.O. France series; 331–7, Index, to both volumes. [Completed from new ser. vol. XVI, with preface covering both volumes.]

Volume XX   C 187

John of Gaunt's Register [Part I, 1371–5]. *Ed*. Sydney Armitage-Smith. Vol. I. R.H.S., 1911. xxv, 350 pp., frontis.

P. v, List of contents [confusing this volume and vol. II]; vii–ix, Preface; xi–xxv, Introduction; 1–350, transcripts in French from first part of Register, chiefly of indentures and other forms of agreement, in Public Record Office, Duchy of Lancaster, Miscellaneous Books no. 13; frontispiece is facsimile of page in Register.

Volume XXI   C 188

John of Gaunt's Register [Part I, 1371–5]. *Ed*. Sydney Armitage-Smith. Vol. II. R.H.S., 1911. [iii], 415 pp., frontis.

Continuing vol. XX. Pp. 1–344, continuation of transcribed entries from Register; 345–57, Appendix containing transcripts of similar items from P.R.O. Chancery, Duchy of Lancaster Miscellanea Bundle IV, P.R.O. Ancient correspondence, and British Museum, Harleian charters and Additional charters; 359–415, Index. Frontispiece is reduced facsimile of letter from William Bacon, mayor of Southampton, to John of Gaunt, 19 Jan. 1376.

Volume XXII   C 189

The official diary of Lieutenant-General Adam Williamson, Deputy-Lieutenant of the Tower of London, 1722–47. *Ed*. John Charles Fox. R.H.S., 1912. [i], 283 pp., frontis.

P. [3], Table of contents; 5–19, Introduction; 21–3, List of the chief officers of the Tower (1688–1750); 25–136, transcript of MS. diary, with notes; 139–254, Appendix, 'Further notes to General Williamson's diary' (p. 139–40, Contents): 44 items, including extracts from documents about famous prisoners mentioned—Bishop Atterbury, Lord Lovat, etc.; 255–83, Index. Frontispiece is reproduction of 'Plan of the Tower of London', 1681–9.

Volume XXIII   C 190

English merchants and the Spanish Inquisition in the Canaries. Extracts from the archives in possession of the Most Hon. the Marquess of Bute. *Ed.* L. de Alberti and A. B. Wallis Chapman. R.H.S., 1912. xviii, 174 pp.

P. iii, Table of contents; v–xi, Introduction, Part I, by L. de Alberti; xii–xviii, Introduction, Part II, by A. B. Wallis Chapman; 1–81, translated extracts from processes of Inquisition in Canary Island and other MSS. (1586–94); 82–152, Spanish text of preceding extracts from processes; 153–9, Appendix, Notes by Wallis Chapman on: trade to Brazil, supply of provisions to heretics, the 'Barbary ambassador', evidence of Hans Anburque, Scottish trade, Bartholomew Cole's confession, Irish trade; 161–74, Index.

Volume XXIV   C 191

Selections from the correspondence of Arthur Capel, Earl of Essex, 1675–7. *Ed.* Clement Edwards Pike. R.H.S., 1913. xv, 162 pp.

Pp. vii–xv, Preface; 1–150, transcripts from B.M. Stowe MSS., with notes, chiefly correspondence and other papers while he was Lord-Lieutenant of Ireland; 151–62, Index.

Volume XXV   C 192

The chronicle of Novgorod, 1016–1471. Translated from the Russian by Robert Michell and Nevill Forbes, with an introduction by C. Raymond Beazley and an account of the text by A. A. Shakhmatov. R.H.S., 1914. xlv, 237 pp.

P. v, Table of contents; vii–xxix, General introduction (on Novgorod); xxx–xxxvi, Notes to the Introduction; xxxvii–xli, An account of the text of the Novgorod chronicle, by Professor A. A. Shakhmatov, St. Petersburg University; xlii, Alphabetical list of titles, technical terms etc. . . . retained in the original Russian, with English equivalents; xliii, Alphabetical list of titles etc. translated; 1–220, translation of chronicle; 221, Appendix (on weights, measurements and currency); 223–4, Note on bibliography; 225–37, Index.

Volume XXVI   C 193

The official papers of Sir Nathaniel Bacon, of Stiffkey, Norfolk, as Justice of the Peace, 1580–1620. Selected and edited, from original papers formerly in the collection of the Marquess Townshend, by H. W. Saunders. R.H.S., 1915. xliii, 255 pp., frontis.

Pp. v–xvi, Table of contents; xxvii–xlii, Introduction; 1–222, transcripts of correspondence, mainly official, and other papers concerning local government in many parts of Norfolk; 223–30, Appendix, 'Ordinances for setting watches on the coast of Norfolk, August 1324'— Latin text, with introductory note; 231–48, Index of names; 249–55, Index of places. Frontispiece is reproduction of drawing of Stiffkey Hall, by Humphrey Repton, 1779. [*Cf. Supplementary Stiffkey papers*, 3rd ser. vol. LII (1936). *See* C 219(*d*) *below*.]

Volume XXVII   C 194

The estate book of Henry de Bray, of Harleston, Co. Northants, *c*. 1289–1340. Edited, from the contemporary MSS., by Dorothy Willis. R.H.S., 1916. xxxix, 159 pp., illus.

P. v, Contents; vi, List of illustrations; vii, Preface; ix–xxx, Introduction; xxxi–xxxix, 'Analysis of the Lansdown [*sic*] and Cotton MSS.', comprising the so-called 'Harlestone register'; 1–132, transcripts in Latin, with marginal annotations; 135–43, pedigrees of de Bray, de Harleston, Dyve and other related families; 145–59, Index. Illustrations: frontispiece, sketch showing remains of Henry de Bray's buildings at Harlestone; p. xxi, reputed effigies of Henry and Mabel de Bray; p. xxii, seal of Ralph Dive, 46 Henry III.

Volume XXVIII   C 195

Autobiography of Thomas Raymond, and memoirs of the family of Guise of Elmore, Gloucestershire. *Ed.* G. Davies. R.H.S., 1917. 184 pp.

P. 3, Preface; 5, Contents; 9–17, Introduction to Raymond's autobiography; 19–66, transcript of autobiography from Bodleian Library, Rawlinson MSS., for years up to 1660, with information about military service in United Provinces, 1633, the Civil War, the State Paper Office, and local affairs; 67–8, Appendix I, Note on the Raymond family (and pedigree); 69–80, Appendix II, Life of Sir William Boswell (uncle of Raymond); 85–99, Memoirs of the family of Guise, Introduction; 102–158, transcript of MS. 'Memoirs of the family of Guise of Elmore, Gloucestershire, written by Sir Christopher Guise and Sir John Guise, barts.'; 159, Appendix I, genealogy of the family of Guise of Elmore; 160, Appendix II, Letter from John Howe to Lord Wharton (2 Aug. 1680); 161–5, Appendix III, Letters on the Cirencester election (1695); 166–77, Appendix IV, Note and transcripts of letters and other documents relating to sequestration of William Guise of Elmore (1644–5); 179–84, Index.

Volume XXIX   C 196

The Stonor letters and papers, 1290–1483. Edited, from the original documents in the Public Record Office, by E. Charles Lethbridge Kingsford. Vol. I. R.H.S., 1919. lvi, 165 pp., frontis., *plus* two folding-in sheets.

> P. v, Contents of vol. I; vii–xlvii, Introduction; xlviii–lvi, Appendix to Introduction, 'The inheritance of Sir Walter de Romesey' (d. 1403); 1–165, transcripts of correspondence and other MSS. of Stonor and connected families in Oxfordshire and Buckinghamshire, 1290–1475. Frontispiece is a map of 'The Stonor country'; genealogy of the Stonor family opp. p. vii; pedigree of 'Sir Walter de Romesey and his descendants', also 'Pedigree alleged by Swete' opp. p. lvi. [Continued by 3rd ser. vol. XXX (1919). *See* C 197 *below*.]

Volume XXX   C 197

The Stonor letters and papers, 1290–1483. *Ed.* C. L. Kingsford. Vol. II. R.H.S., 1919. v, 224 pp., frontis.

> P. v, Contents of vol. II; 1–163, transcripts continued from 1475/6–1483; 165–91, Appendix, viz. pp. 165–70, I, Calendar of 'Miscellaneous Stonor MSS.' in P.R.O.; 171–6, II, List of 'Stonor deeds'; 177–82, III, List of 'Stonor estate accounts'; 183–4, IV, List of rentals; 184, V, 'Court rolls of Stonor manors at the Public Record Office'; 185–6, VI, 'Addenda to miscellaneous Stonor MSS.' (above); 186–7, note and text of the will of Edmund Stonor (? 1475); 188–91, 'Index to letters in Ancient Correspondence [P.R.O.] printed in these volumes'; 191, 'Stonor letters in other volumes of Ancient Correspondence'; 192–200, Glossary; 201, Latin legal terms; 202–16, Index of persons; 217–24, Index of places. Frontispiece is facsimile of signatures from the Stonor papers. [The two vols. are supplemented by C 201(*b*) *below*.]

Volume XXXI   C 198

The Nicholas papers. Correspondence of Sir Edward Nicholas, Secretary of State. *Ed.* Sir George F. Warner. Vol. IV, 1657–60. R.H.S., 1920. xxix, 283 pp.

> Pp. v–xix, Preface; 1–268, texts; 269–83, Index. [Continuation of new ser. vols. XL, L and LVII. *See* C 145, C 155, C 162 *above*.]

Volume XXXII   C 199

British diplomatic instructions, 1689–1789. Vol. I, Sweden, 1689–1727. *Ed.* James Frederick Chance. R.H.S., 1922. xxxviii, 250 pp.

> Pp. v–vii, Preface (explaining the series); ix–xxxviii, Introduction; 1–243, annotated transcripts from Public Record Office, of general instructions issued to British envoys to Sweden and others concerned, viz. pp. 1–13,

William Duncombe (1689–92); 14–38, Dr. John Robinson (1692–1709); 39–65, Robert Jackson and James Jefferyes (1709–14); 66–73, Jackson, Jefferyes and others (1714–15); 74–104, 'The Baltic expeditions (1715–1718)'; 105–40, Lord Carteret (1719–20); 141–69, William Finch (1720–24); 170–243, Stephen Poyntz (1724–7); 245–50, Index. Continued by C 206 *below*.

Volume XXXIII
C 200

Parliamentary papers of John Robinson, 1774–84. *Ed.* William Thomas Laprade. R.H.S., 1922. xx, 198 pp.

> Pp. v–xx, Introduction; 1–173, copies of transcripts made by B. F. Stevens from Robinson papers, arranged as follows: 3–27, Section I, The Parliamentary election of 1774; 31–62, Section II, The election of 1780; 65–132, Section III, The election of 1784; 135–73, Section IV, Secret and special service accounts; 175–86, Appendix I, extracts from Robinson's letters to Henry Nevill, on his candidature for Monmouthshire, 1783–4; 181–91, Appendix II, text of report by B. F. Stevens 7 July 1892, on the Robinson papers at Eridge Castle; 193–8, Index.

Volume XXXIV
C 201

Camden Miscellany, Vol. XIII. R.H.S., 1924. In five sections separately paged, viz.

(*a*) *Gesta Dunelmensia, A.D. M°.CCC°.* Edited from a manuscript in the Treasury of the Dean and Chapter of Durham by Robert K. Richardson. R.H.S., 1924. xiv, 58 pp.

> Pp. v–xiv, Introduction; 1–53, Latin text; 55–8, Index.

(*b*) Supplementary Stonor letters and papers, 1314–1482. *Ed.* C. L. Kingsford. R.H.S., 1924. viii, 26 pp.

> Supplementing C 196, C 197 *above*. Pp. v–viii, Introduction; 1–22, texts in Latin, French and English, with explanatory notes and calendar of less important documents; 23–6, Index.

(*c*) Devereux papers, with Richard Broughton's memoranda, 1575–1601. *Ed.* Henry Elliot Malden. R.H.S., 1923. xii, 36 pp.

> Pp. v–x, Introduction; xi–xii, Table of contents; 1–33, texts; 35–6, Index.

(*d*) The voyages of Captain William Jackson, 1642–5. *Ed.* Vincent T. Harlow. R.H.S., 1923. xxvi, 39 pp.

> Pp. v–xxvi, Introduction; 1–35, Text of *A Briefe Journall or a Succinct and true relation of the most Remarkable Passages observed in that Voyage undertaken by Captaine William Jackson to the Westerne Indies or Continent of America, Anno Domini* 1642, with explanatory notes; 37–9, Index.

(*e*) The English conquest of Jamaica. An account of what happened in the island of Jamaica, from May 20 of the year 1655, when the English laid siege to it, up to July 3 of the year 1656, by Captain Julian de Castilla. Translated from the original MS. in the Archives of the Indies and edited . . . by Irene A. Wright. R.H.S., 1923. vi, 32 pp.

Pp. v–vi, Introduction; 1–29, translated text; 31–2, Index.

Volume XXXV   C 202

British diplomatic instructions, 1689–1789. Vol. II, France, 1689–1721. *Ed.* L. G. Wickham Legg. R.H.S., 1925. xxxviii, 212 pp.

Pp. v–ix, Preface; xi–xxxviii, Introduction; 1–182, annotated transcripts from P.R.O., Foreign Entry Books, King's Letters, Regencies and State Papers France series, of instructions issued to ambassadors and other British representatives in France, viz. 1–3, Earl of Portland (1697–8); 4, Earl of Jersey (1698–9); 5–7, Earl of Manchester (1699–1701); 8–23, Duke of Marlborough and Viscount Townshend (1709–10); 24, Matthew Prior (1711); 25–7, Viscount Bolingbroke and Prior (1712); 28–33, Bishop of Bristol and Earl of Strafford (1712–13); 34–79, Prior (1712–15) and Duke of Shrewsbury (1712–13); 80–172, Earl of Stair (1714–20); 173–82, Sir Robert Sutton (1720–21); 183–205, Appendix, 'King's Instructions to Commissioners', extracts and notes on those issued concerning the commercial treaty of 1713, to General Charles Ross in 1714, on the demolition of Dunkirk, on colonial questions, particularly frontiers in North America; 207–12, Index. Supplemented and continued by C 205, C 210, C 216 *below.*

Volume XXXVI   C 203

British diplomatic instructions 1689–1789. Vol. III, Denmark. *Ed.* James Frederick Chance. R.H.S., 1926. xli, 229 pp.

Pp. v–vi, Preface; vii–xli, Introduction; 1–219, annotated transcripts from P.R.O. Foreign Entry Books, F.O. Denmark etc. of instructions to following representatives: 1–21, Robert Molesworth, Thomas Fotherby, Hugh Greg and Lord Lexington (1689–1701); 22–44, James Vernon and Daniel Pulteney (1702–15); 45–60, Lord Polwarth (1716–1721); 61–88, Lord Glenorchy (1721–30); 89–164, Walter Titley (1729–1768); 165–81, Dudley Cosby and Robert Gunning (1764–71); 182–91, Robert Murray Keith, Ralph Woodford and Daniel de Laval (1771–9); 192–219, Morton Eden and Hugh Elliot (1779–89); 221–9, Index.

Volume XXXVII   C 204

Camden Miscellany, Vol. XIV. R.H.S., 1926. In five sections separately paged, viz.

(*a*) Spanish narratives of the English attack on Santo Domingo, 1655. Transcribed and translated from the original documents in the General Archives of the Indies and edited for the Royal Historical Society by I. A. Wright. R.H.S., 1926. xiii, 80 pp., frontis. (plan of Santo Domingo, etc. 1656).

Pp. vii–xiii, Introduction; 1–67, translated texts; 68–76, Appendices— Supplementary documents and key to plan and notes (73–6) on frontispiece; 77–80, Index.

(*b*) *Embajada Española*. An anonymous contemporary Spanish guide to diplomatic procedure in the last quarter of the seventeenth century. Translated and edited by H. J. Chaytor. R.H.S., 1926. xi, 46 pp.

Pp. v–xi, Preface; 1–43, Spanish text and parallel translation; 45–6, Index.

(*c*) The will of Peter de Aqua Blanca, bishop of Hereford, 1268. *Ed.* C. Eveleigh Woodruff. R.H.S., 1926. xi, 13 pp.

Pp. v–xi, Preface; 1–9, Latin text; 11–13, Index.

(*d*) The ransom of John II, King of France, 1360–70. *Ed.* Dorothy M. Broome. R.H.S., 1926. xxvi, 44 pp.

Pp. vii–xxvi, Preface; 1–38, Latin and French texts (two additional folded-in sheets between pp. 10 and 11); 39–44, Index.

(*e*) *Historia siue Narracio de modo et forma Mirabilis Parliamenti apud Westmonasterium anno domini millesimo CCCLXXXVI, regni vero regis Ricardi Secundi post Conquestum anno decimo, per Thomam Fauent clericum indictata.* Edited from a manuscript in the Bodleian Library by May McKisack. R.H.S., 1926. viii, 27 pp.

Pp. v–viii, Preface; 1–24, Latin text; 25–7, Index.

Volume XXXVIII   C 205

British diplomatic instructions, 1689–1789. Vol. IV, France, 1721–7. *Ed.* L. G. Wickham Legg. R.H.S., 1927. xlii, 253 pp.

Continuing C 202 *above*. P. v, Preface; vii–xl, Introduction; xli–xlii, *Addenda* to vol II (Instructions to Lord Portland, 8 Jan. 1698, and to Robert Sutton, 18 Nov. 1720); 1–245, annotated transcripts mostly from British Museum, Carteret, Newcastle and Townshend Papers, also P.R.O. State Papers, France etc. of instructions to British representatives, viz. 1–46, Sir Robert Sutton (1720–1) and Sir Luke Schaub (1721–1724); 47–245, Horatio Walpole (1723–7); 247–53, Index. Continued by C 210 and C 216.

Volume XXXIX   C 206

British diplomatic instructions, 1689–1789. Vol. V, Sweden, 1727–89. *Ed.* James Frederick Chance. R.H.S., 1928. xxvi, 268 pp.

Continuing C 199. Pp. v–vi, Preface; vii–xxvi, Introduction; 1–260, annotated transcripts, mostly from P.R.O. State Papers Sweden and B.M. Titley, Gunning and other papers of envoys, giving instructions to British representatives, viz. pp. 1–4, Isaac Leheup and Baron von Diescau (1727–8); 5–78, Edward Finch (1728–39); 79–88, John Burnaby (1739–41); 89–129, Melchior Guy Dickens (1742–8); 130–2, Robert Campbell (1757); 133–226, Sir John Goodricke, bart. (1758–73); 227–33, Lewis de Visme and J. L. Doerfeld (1774–8); 234–60, Sir Thomas Wroughton and Charles Keene (1778–89); 261–8, Index.

Volume XL   C 207

The *Vita Wulfstani* of William of Malmesbury, to which are added the extant abridgments of this work, and the Miracles and Translation of St. Wulfstan. *Ed.* Reginald R. Darlington. R.H.S., 1928. lii, 204 pp.

Pp. v–vi, Preface; vii–lii, Introduction; 1–67, transcript of text in Latin of William of Malmesbury's Life of Wulfstan, as preserved in British Museum, MS. Cott. Claud. A.v with marginal synopsis and footnotes; 68–114, 'The abridgment of William of Malmesbury's Life of Wulfstan in MS. B.iv, 39*b* of the library of the dean and chapter of Durham, collated with MSS. Harl. 322 (H.) and Lansd. 436 (R.) in the British Museum' (Latin texts, with notes); 115–88, transcript of 'The miracles of St. Wulfstan' from MS. B.iv, 39*b* in the library of the dean and chapter of Durham; 189–91, Appendix, List of documents relating to Wulfstan; 193–204, Index.

Volume XLI   C 208

The Camden Miscellany, Vol. XV. R.H.S., 1929. In six sections, separately paged, viz.

(*a*) A transcript of 'The red book', a detailed account of the Hereford bishopric estates in the thirteenth century. *Ed.* A. T. Bannister. R.H.S., 1929. ix, 36 pp.

Pp. v–ix, Introduction; 1–33, transcript in Latin; 35–6, Index.

(*b*) Edward II, the Lords Ordainers and Piers Gaveston's jewels and horses, 1312–13. *Ed.* R. A. Roberts. R.H.S., 1929. viii, 26 pp.

Pp. v–viii, Introduction; 1–22, copy of a transcript in Latin from a roll in the Vatican concerning the recovery by Edward of the jewels by Papal intervention; 23–6, Index.

(*c*) Table of Canterbury archbishopric charters. Transcribed and edited by Irene J. Churchill. R.H.S., 1929. x, 27 pp.

Pp. v–x, Introduction; 1–19, transcript of MS. in Public Record Office, Miscellaneous Books of the Exchequer, Treasury of Receipt, E36/137; 21–7, Index.

(*d*) An early Admiralty case, A.D. 1361. *Ed.* Charles Johnson. [No title page.]

Pp. 1–2, Introductory note; 2–5, transcript of document in French illustrating law of the sea, from P.R.O. Chancery Miscellanea, Bundle 6.

(*e*) Select tracts and table books relating to English weights and measures, 1100–1742. *Ed.* Hubert Hall and Frieda J. Nicholas. R.H.S., 1929. xviii, 68 pp.

P. vii, Preface; ix–xiv, Introduction; xv–xviii, List of tracts and table books; 1–53, extracts from the MSS. listed; 55–8, Appendix, 'List of authorities'; 59–68, Index.

(*f*) An English prisoner in Paris during the Terror, 1793–4. *Ed.* V. T. Harlow. [No separate title page.]

Pp. 1–3, Introductory note; 3–10, transcript from Codrington MSS. of account probably written by Sir William Codrington, 3rd bart.

Volume XLII   C 209

Notes of the debates in the House of Lords officially taken by Robert Bowyer and Henry Elsing, clerks of the parliaments, A.D. 1621, 1625, 1628. Edited from the original manuscripts in the Inner Temple Library, the Bodleian Library and House of Lords by Frances Helen Relf. R.H.S., 1929. xxxii, 239 pp.

Pp. v–vii, Preface; ix–xxxii, Introduction; 1–212, transcripts, with footnotes, of four 'scribbled books' recording debates kept by the clerks and assistant clerks of the Parliament; 213–29, Appendix, transcript of the scribbled book of Henry Elsing's son for June 1628; 231–9, Index.

Volume XLIII   C 210

British diplomatic instructions, 1689–1789. Vol. VI, France, 1727–44. *Ed.* L. G. Wickham Legg. R.H.S., 1930. xl, 255 pp.

Continued from C 205 *above*. Pp. v–vii, Preface; viii–xl, Introduction; 1–242, annotated transcripts from Public Record Office and Newcastle Papers, British Museum, of general instructions to British representatives in France, viz. pp. 1–25, Horatio Walpole (1727–30); 26–82, William Stanhope (later Lord Harrington), H. Walpole and Stephen Poyntz (1728–30); 83–239, James, Earl Waldegrave (1730–40); 239–42, Anthony Thompson (1740–43/4); 243–8, Appendix, Instructions for

John Armstrong as commissary to Dunkirk (18 July 1728), and Thomas Lascelles (6 March 1729/30); 249–55, Index. [Continued by C 216 *below*.]

Volume XLIV   C 211

Private correspondence of Chesterfield and Newcastle, 1744–1746. Part I, Chesterfield at the Hague. Part 2, Chesterfield at Dublin. Edited, with an introduction and notes, by Sir Richard Lodge. R.H.S., 1930. xlv, 155 pp.

P. v, Preface; vii, List of contents; ix–xlv, Introduction; 1–140, transcripts of correspondence from British Museum, Newcastle Papers: 1–58, Part I, Dec. 1744 to May 1745, Chesterfield at the Hague; 61–140, Part II, Aug. 1745 to Oct. 1746, Chesterfield at Dublin (including a few letters written in England); 141–2, Appendix A, Letter in French from Frederick II of Prussia to Andrié (7 March 1746); 143–5, Appendix B, extract of letter from Newcastle to Cumberland (23 May 1746), and his letter to Stephen Poyntz (23 May 1746); 146–7, Appendix C, letter from Newcastle to Hardwicke (28 Oct. 1746); 149–55, Index.

Volume XLV   C 212

Documents illustrating the activities of the general and provincial chapters of the English Black Monks, 1215–1540. *Ed.* William Abel Pantin. [Vol. I]. R.H.S., 1931. xvii, 296 pp.

P. v, Contents; vii–ix, Preface; xi–xvii, Introduction, including list of monastic registers or letter-books of the period; 1–271, annotated transcripts in Latin from various sources, arranged as follows: 1–213, Part I, 'General chapters of the province of Canterbury, 1215–1336' (texts, with explanatory introductions), e.g. 3–6, 'Note on the General Chapter'; 217–71, Part II, 'General chapters of the province of York, 1215–1336' (217–32, note on 'The records of the Northern chapters'); 273–6, Appendix I, 'The decretals *In singulis regnis* and *Ea quae*' (texts); 277–280, Appendix II, 'Note on the extracts from the Norwich rolls'; 281–7, Appendix III, Comparative table of the statutes of the Southern province; 289–91, Appendix IV, Comparative table of the statutes of the Northern and Southern chapters; 293–6, Appendix V, Chronological table of chapters and presidents, with references to the relevant documents. [Continued by C 214 and C 221 *below*.]

Volume XLVI   C 213

British diplomatic representatives, 1689–1789. *Ed.* D. B. Horn. R.H.S., 1932. xiii, 178 pp.

Pp. vii–viii, Preface; ix–xi, Introduction; xiii, List of abbreviations; 1–168, Lists of representatives; 169–78, Index of persons.

Volume XLVII   C 214

Documents illustrating the activities of the general and provincial chapters of the English Black Monks, 1215–1540. Vol. II. *Ed.* William Abel Pantin. R.H.S., 1933. xix, 232 pp.

> Continued from C 212 *above*. Pp. v–xix, Introduction; 1–226, texts in Latin of 'Acts and statutes of the provincial chapters of the English province, 1336–1540', with notes; 227–9, Appendix I, table showing relationship of statutes; 230–2, Appendix II, Summary of papal constitutions for reform of Black Monks, 1336. Continued by C 221 *below*.

Volume XLVIII   C 215

The diplomatic correspondence of Richard II. *Ed.* Edouard Perroy. R.H.S., 1933. xxxii, 281 pp., frontis. (fac. letter).

> Pp. vii–xxxii, Introduction; 1–175, Latin or Old French texts of correspondence, some calendaring in English, 1377–99; 176–9, Appendix, Undated letters; 180–256, Historical notes; 257–81, Index.

Volume XLIX   C 216

British diplomatic instructions, 1689–1789. Vol. VII, France, Part IV, 1745–89. *Ed.* L. G. Wickham Legg. R.H.S., 1934. xxxiii, 338 pp.

> Continuing C 202, C 205 and C 210 *above*. Pp. vii–ix, Preface; xi–xxxiii, Introduction; 1–327, annotated transcripts, from Public Record Office, Newcastle Papers in the British Museum and Sackville Papers, of instructions to British representatives abroad, viz. pp. 1–52, William Anne Keppel, 2nd earl of Albemarle (1749–54); 53–4, Hans Stanley (1761); 55–83, John Russell, 4th duke of Bedford (1762–3); 84–92, Francis Seymour-Conway, earl of Hertford (1763–5); 93–7, Charles Lennox, 3rd duke of Richmond (1765–6); 98–106, William Henry Nassau de Zuylestein, 4th earl of Rochford (1766–8); 107–27, Simon Harcourt, 1st Earl Harcourt (1768–72); 128–77, David Murray, 7th Viscount Stormont (1772–8); 178, Thomas Grenville (1782); 179–228, Alleyne Fitzherbert (1782–3); 229–47, George Montagu, 4th duke of Manchester (1783); 248–306, John Frederick Sackville, 3rd duke of Dorset (1784–9); 307–27, Appendix: 307–13, I, 'Instructions on questions in the Colonies 1750': 313–15, II, Despatch on Dunkirk (8 Nov. 1773): 315–27, III, 'Instructions and despatches on the trade negociations' (commercial treaty of 1786); 329–38, Index.

Volume L   C 217

British diplomatic representatives, 1789–1852. *Ed.* S. T. Bindoff, E. F. Malcolm Smith and C. K. Webster. R.H.S., 1934. xvii, 216 pp.

Pp. ix–x, Preface, by C. K. Webster; xi–xv, Introduction, by S. T. Bindoff; xvii, list of abbreviations; 1–198, annotated lists of representatives; 199–216, Index of persons.

Volume LI   C 218

Rotuli Parliamentorum Anglie hactenus inediti, MCCLXXIX–MCCCLXXIII. *Ed.* H. G. Richardson and George Sayles. R.H.S., 1935. xxxii, 337 pp.

Pp. vii–xxviii, Introduction, I The development of Parliament, II Parliamentary records, III The publication of the Parliament rolls; xxix–xxxiii, Table of Parliament rolls of Edward I, Edward II and Edward III; 1–281, Latin, Old French and English texts, with explanatory notes; 283–6, Appendix, Parliament at Westminster, Epiphany-Candlemas (1327); 287, Table of references to manuscripts; 288–94, Glossary of Old French; 295–323, Index of persons and places; 324–37, Index of subjects.

Volume LII   C 219

Camden Miscellany, Vol. XVI. R.H.S., 1936. In five sections separately paged, viz.

(*a*) *The state of England anno dom. 1600.* By Thomas Wilson. Edited from the manuscripts among the State Papers in the Public Record Office by F. J. Fisher. R.H.S., 1936. vii, 47 pp.

Pp. v–vii, Introduction; 1–43, text; 45–7, Index.

(*b*) *Discours of the Turkes.* By Sr. Thomas Sherley. *Ed.* E. Denison Ross. R.H.S., 1936. ix, 45 pp.

Pp. v–ix, Introduction; 1–39, text; 41–5, Index.

(*c*) A relation of a short survey of the western counties, made by a lieutenant of the military company in Norwich in 1635. *Ed.* L. G. Wickham Legg. R.H.S., 1936. xiv, 128 pp.

Pp. iii–xiv, Introduction; 1–97, text; 99–118, notes; 119–28, Index.

(*d*) Supplementary Stiffkey papers. *Ed.* F. W. Brooks. R.H.S., 1936. xviii, 55 pp. [Further papers of Sir Nathaniel Bacon, supplementing Camden 3rd ser. XXVI (1915). *See* C 193 *above.*]

Pp. v–xviii, Introduction; 1–52, texts; 53–5, Index.

(*e*) A probate inventory of goods and chattels of Sir John Eliot, late prisoner in the Tower, 1633. *Ed.* Harold Hulme. R.H.S., 1936. viii, 15 pp.

Pp. v–viii, Introduction; 1–14, text; 15, Index.

Volume LIII C 220

Robert Loder's farm accounts, 1610–20. *Ed.* G. E. Fussell. R.H.S., 1936. xxxi, 207 pp., frontispiece (facsimile of an account), folding table.

Pp. vii–xxxi, Introduction, including four tables; 1–189, text; 191–5, Appendix, Terrier of church lands, buildings etc. at Harwell, Berks., 1634; 197–8, Glossary; 199–207, Index.

Volume LIV C 221

Documents illustrating the activities of the General and Provincial Chapters of the English Black Monks, 1215–1540. Vol. III. *Ed.* William Abel Pantin. R.H.S., 1937. ix, 414 pp.

Continued from C 212 and C 214 *above*. P. ix, Preface; 1–136, Part II, Miscellaneous documents concerning the provincial chapters, 1336–1540, Documents nos. 181–284; 137–94, Part III, Financial documents, 1336–1540; 195–253, Part IV, Proxies, visitation citations and certificates, 1336–1540; 255–7, Appendix I, Illustrative extracts from monastic accounts; 258, Appendix II, Table of contributions; 259–62, Table of chapters and presidents, with references to the relevant documents; 263–312, *Addenda* and *corrigenda* [to Vols. I and II]; 313–16, Index of MSS. referred to; 317–24, Index of selected biographies; 325–74, Index of persons and places; 375–414, Index of subjects [Indexes are to all three volumes].

Volume LV C 222

Memorials of the Holles family, 1493–1656. By Gervase Holles. Edited from the manuscripts at Longleat and Welbeck by A. C. Wood. R.H.S., 1937. xiv, 287 pp.

Pp. vii–xiv, Introduction; 1–236, text; 237–66, Notes; 267–86, Index.

Volume LVI C 223

John of Gaunt's Register, 1379–83. Vol. I. Edited from the original record by the late Eleanor C. Lodge and Robert Somerville. 1937. Pp. i–1, 1–233.

Pp. vii–viii, Preface, by (Sir) R. Somerville; ix–1, Introduction mainly by Miss Lodge; 1–233, French and Latin texts, with calendaring in English of entries which are in standard form. Continued by C 224 *below*.

Volume LVII C 224

John of Gaunt's Register, 1379–83. Vol. II. *Ed.* Eleanor C. Lodge and Robert Somerville. R.H.S., 1937. Pp. i–vi, 235–489.

P. vi, *Corrigenda*, vols. I and II; pp. 235–412, French and Latin texts and calendaring continued from Vol. I; 413–16, Appendix I, A, Collation of the enrolment with original documents in P.L.3/1 (Public Record Office), B, Writs under the duke of Lancaster's privy seal not enrolled in the register; 417–18, Appendix II, *Addenda*; 419–20, Appendix III, Glossary; 421–89, Index to both volumes.

Volume LVIII

C 225

Early charters of the cathedral church of St. Paul, London. *Ed*. Marion Gibbs. R.H.S., 1939. [v], xlviii, 338 pp.

Pp. i–iv, Preface by (Sir) F. M. Stenton; v, Editor's preface; vii–xlviii, Introduction; 1–277, Anglo-Saxon, Latin texts, including earlier part of *Liber Pilosus*, with explanatory headings; 279–80, Appendix, 'Calendar of chapters in Liber A . . .'; 281–327, Index nominum et locorum; 328–338, Index rerum.

Volume LIX

C 226

The formation of Canning's Ministry, February to August 1827. Edited from contemporary correspondence by Arthur Aspinall. R.H.S., 1937. lvii, 327 pp.

P. vii, List of sources; ix–xi, List of ministers; xiii–xxvi, List of letters; xxv–liv, Introduction; lv–lvii, Note on Canning's financial position; 1–300, texts of correspondence; 301–12, Select bibliography; 313–27, Index.

Volume LX

C 227

The correspondence of Lord Aberdeen and Princess Lieven, 1832–54. Vol. I, 1832–48. *Ed*. E. Jones Parry. R.H.S., 1938. Pp. i–xxi, 1–291.

Pp. ix–xxi, Introduction; 1–291, texts of correspondence in English and French. Continued by C 229 *below*.

Volume LXI

C 228

The letters of Arnulf of Lisieux. *Ed*. Frank Barlow. R.H.S., 1939. xc, 236 pp.

Pp. ix–x, List of abbreviations; xi–xc, Introduction; 1–217, texts in Latin; 219–20, Index of incipits; 221–36, Index of persons and places.

Volume LXII

C 229

The correspondence of Lord Aberdeen and Princess Lieven, 1832–54. Vol. II, 1848–54. *Ed*. E. Jones Parry. R.H.S., 1939. Pp. i–vii, 293–669.

Continued from C 227 *above*. Pp. 293–654, Texts of correspondence in English and French; 655–69, Index to both volumes.

Volume LXIII

C 230

British consular reports on the trade and politics of Latin America, 1824–6. *Ed.* R. A. Humphreys. R.H.S., 1940. xxii, 385 pp. + three folding tables opposite pp. 56, 60 and 206, folding map at end.

> Pp. vii–xiv, Introduction; xv–xvii, List of documents; xviii–xix, List of consuls; xx, Glossary; xxi, Currency, weights and measures; xxii, Abbreviations; 1–342, Texts of reports; 344–9, Appendix I A, Exports in pounds sterling of British and Irish goods from Great Britain to Latin America (1812–30); 350–1, I B, Exports in pounds sterling of foreign and and colonial merchandise from Great Britain to Latin America (1812–1830); 352–3, Appendix II, Note on Spanish commercial reforms in the eighteenth century; 354, Appendix III A, List of manuscripts cited; 354–9, III B, List of references; 361–85, Index; folding map of Latin America in 1826.

Volume LXIV

C 231

Camden Miscellany, Vol. XVII. R.H.S., 1940. In three sections separately paged, viz.

(*a*) Ely chapter ordinances and Visitation records, 1241–1515. *Ed.* Seiriol J. A. Evans. R.H.S., 1940. xx, 74 pp.

> Pp. v–xx, Introduction; 1–67, texts in Latin; 69–74, Index.

(*b*) Mr. Harrie Cavendish his journey to and from Constantinople 1589. By Fox, his servant. *Ed.* A. C. Wood. R.H.S., 1940. x, 29 pp., portrait.

> Pp. iii–x, Introduction; 1–25, text; 27–9, Index.

(*c*) Sir John Eliot and the Vice-Admiralty of Devon. *Ed.* Harold Hulme. R.H.S., 1940. xiv, 56 pp.

> Pp. v–xiv, Introduction; 1–51, texts of: A, Sir John Eliot's personal accounts (1622–5); B, Eliot's accounts in Admiralty records; C, Depositions taken in 1627; D, Brief of evidence against Sir John Eliot (1627); 53–6, Index.

Volume LXV

C 232

The correspondence of Charles Arbuthnot. *Ed.* A. Aspinall. R.H.S., 1941. xviii, 268 pp. + folding genealogical table.

> Pp. vii–xviii, Introduction; 1–254, texts of correspondence; 255–68, Index.

Volume LXVI

C 233

Ministers' Accounts of the Earldom of Cornwall, 1296–7. Vol. I. *Ed.* L. Margaret Midgley. 1942. xxxix, 150 pp.

Pp. vii–xxxvii, Introduction; xxxviii–xxxix, 'Some manuscript sources, preserved in the Public Record Office, for a survey of the lands of the earldom of Cornwall, 1272–1300'; 1–150, Latin text. Continued by C 235 *below.*

Volume LXVII   C 234

The notebook of John Penry, 1593. Edited . . . from the original in the Huntington Library by Albert Peel. 1944. xxviii, 99 pp. + 2 facsimiles.

Pp. vii–xxv, Introduction; xxvii–xxviii, Contents in Notebook order; 1–97, Text in 13 Sections, with explanatory headings to each; 98–9, Index.

Volume LXVIII   C 235

Ministers' Accounts of the Earldom of Cornwall, 1296–7. Vol. II. *Ed.* L. Margaret Midgley. 1945. Pp. i–vi, 151–342. *plus erratum* slip.

Continued from C 233 *above.* Pp. v–vi, *Corrigenda*; 151–277, Latin text continued from Vol. LXVI; 279–80, Glossary; 281–342, Index of persons and places.

Volume LXIX   C 236

The Letter-book of John Viscount Mordaunt 1658–60. *Ed.* Mary Coate. 1945. xxiv, 196 pp., frontis.

Pp. vii–xxiii, Introduction; 1–182, text; 183–4, Appendix, 'Sir Richard Willis'; 185–96, Index. Frontispiece is repro. of engraved portrait of Lord Mordaunt.

Volume LXX   C 237

The Gascon Calendar of 1322. Edited from Miscellaneous Books, Exchequer Treasury of Receipt, Vol. 187, in the Public Record Office, by G. P. Cuttino. 1949. xvii, 202 pp. + 2 plates.

Pp. vii–xii, Introduction; xiii–xiv, List of abbreviations; xiii–xvii, Contents of the calendar; 1–166, Latin text; 167–202, Index of persons and places. Two plates illustrate pressmarks.

Volume LXXI   C 238

Cartulary of St. Mary Clerkenwell. *Ed.* W. O. Hassall. R.H.S., 1949. xxii, 358 pp.

Pp. vii–xviii, Introduction; xix–xx, Chronological list of deeds; xxi, Note on transcription and editing; xxii, List of abbreviations; 1–274, Documents in Latin, with explanatory headings; 275–7, Appendix 1, Documents not included in the cartulary; 278, Appendix 2, Surnames in the cartulary; 279–80, Appendix 3, The cartulary and the early topography and history of London; 281–3, Appendix 4, The chronology of the prioresses; 284–6, Appendix 5, Topographical summary of nunnery properties; 287–90, Appendix 6, List of manuscript sources; 291–344, Index 1, Persons and places; 345–58, Index 2, Subjects.

Volume LXXII   C 239

Encomium Emmae Reginae. Ed. Alistair Campbell. R.H.S., 1949. lxix, 108 pp.

Pp. xi–lxix, Introduction; 3, 'On the text and textual notes'; 4–53, Latin text and parallel English translation; 55–61, Appendix I, Queen Emma's name, title and forms of assent; 62–5, Appendix II, The status of Queen Emma and her predecessors; 66–91, Appendix III, The Scandinavian supporters of Knútr; 92–3, Appendix IV, Text of the supplement to *Jómsvíkinga Saga* [in normalized Old Norse spelling]; 94–8, Appendix V, Additional notes; 99, Postscript, Ove Moberg's *Olav Haraldsson, Knut den Store och Sverige* (Lund, 1941); 100–3, General Index; 104–5, Index to the text of the *Encomium*; 106–8, Glossary.

Volume LXXIII   C 240

Select documents of the English lands of the Abbey of Bec. *Ed.* Marjorie Chibnall. R.H.S., 1951. xvii, 213 pp.

Pp. ix–xv, Introduction; xvii, List of abbreviations; 1–185, Latin texts of charters, custumals and account rolls; 187–8, Glossary; 189–207, Index I, Persons and places; 208–13, Index II, Subjects.

Volume LXXIV   C 241

The *Anglica historia* of Polydore Vergil, A.D. 1485–1537. Edited with a translation by Denys Hay. R.H.S., 1950. xlii, 373 pp.

Pp. ix–xlii, Introduction; 1, List of abbreviations; 2–337, text in Latin with parallel English translation; 339–73, Index.

Volume LXXV   C 242

The correspondence of David Scott, director and chairman of the East India Company, relating to Indian affairs, 1787–1805. *Ed.* C. H. Philips. Vol. I, 1787–99. R.H.S., 1951. Pp. i–xxviii, 1–228, frontispiece (portrait).

Pp. ix–xxii, Introduction; xxiii–xxviii, Table of letters in volume I; 1–228, texts of correspondence. Continued by C 243 *below*.

Volume LXXVI   C 243

The correspondence of David Scott, director and chairman of the East India Company, relating to Indian affairs, 1787–1805.

Ed. C. H. Philips. Vol. II, 1800–05. R.H.S., 1950. Pp. i–xii, 229–458.

> Continued from C 242 *above.* Pp. viii–xii, Table of letters in volume II; 229–446, Texts; 447–58, Index.

Volume LXXVII

C 244

The private correspondence of Lord Macartney, governor of Madras, 1781–5. *Ed.* C. Collin Davies. R.H.S., 1950. xxiv, 236 pp.

> Pp. vii–xix, Introduction; xxi–xxiv, Chronological table of letters; 1–228, Texts; 229–30, Glossary; 231–6, Index.

Volume LXXVIII

C 245

The despatches of Sir Robert Sutton, ambassador in Constantinople, 1710–14. *Ed.* Akdes Nimet Kurat. 1953. [v], 220 pp.

> Pp. 1–12, Introduction; 13–206, texts in English, French and Italian; 207–10, Glossary of Turkish titles and expressions; 211–20, Index.

Volume LXXIX

C 246

Camden Miscellany, Vol. XVIII. R.H.S., 1948. In three sections separately paged, viz.

(*a*) The Benares diary of Warren Hastings. *Ed.* C. Collin Davies. R.H.S., 1948. viii, 39 pp.

> Pp. v–viii, Introduction; 1–36, Text; 37–38, Appendix, 'Treaty with the Nawab-Vizier Shujah-ul-Dowla, 7 September 1773'; 39–40, Index.

(*b*) Some letters of the Duke of Wellington to his brother, William Wellesley-Pole. *Ed.* Sir Charles Webster. R.H.S., 1948. vii, 38 pp.

> Pp. v–vii, Introduction; 1–38, texts of correspondence, 1807–17.

(*c*) The Restoration Visitation of the university of Oxford and its colleges. *Ed.* F. J. Varley. R.H.S., 1948. x, 64 pp.

> Pp. v–x, Introduction; 1–56, text of Visitation register (1660–2); 57, List of Commissioners; 58–64, Index.

Volume LXXX

C 247

Camden Miscellany, Vol. XIX. R.H.S., 1952. In two sections, separately paged, viz.

(*a*) Some documents regarding the fulfilment and interpretation of the Treaty of Brétigny, 1361–9. *Ed*. Pierre Chaplais. R.H.S., 1952. 84 pp.

> Part I: pp. 5–8, Introduction, Anglo-French negotiations of 1361–2; 9–50, texts in French and Latin. Part II: The opinions of the doctors of Bologna on the sovereignty of Aquitaine (1369), a source of the *Songe du Verger*: pp. 51–7, Introduction; 58–78, transcripts in Latin; 79–84, Index of persons and places.

(*b*) The Anglo-French negotiations at Bruges, 1374–7. *Ed*. Edouard Perroy. R.H.S., 1952. xix, 95 pp.

> Pp. v–xix, Introduction, including (xix) Note on the transcription; 1–68, texts in French and Latin; 69–85, Appendix including instructions to French ambassadors, 1372 and 1377; 87–95, Index.

Volume LXXXI   C 248

The political correspondence of Mr. Gladstone and Lord Granville, 1868–76. *Ed*. Agatha Ramm. Vol. I, 1868–71. R.H.S., 1952. Pp. i–xix, 1–246.

> Pp. ix–xviii, Introduction; 1–246, texts. Continued by C 249 *below*.

Volume LXXXII   C 249

The political correspondence of Mr. Gladstone and Lord Granville, 1868–76. *Ed*. Agatha Ramm. Vol. II, 1871–6. R.H.S., 1952. Pp. i–v, 247–518.

> Continuing C 248. Pp. 247–490, texts; 491–518, Index to both volumes.

Volume LXXXIII   C 250

Camden Miscellany, Vol. XX. R.H.S., 1953. In three sections separately paged, viz.

(*a*) *A Briefe Collection of the Queenes Majesties Most High and Most Honourable Courtes of Recordes*. By Richard Robinson. *Ed*. R. L. Rickard. R.H.S., 1953. vi, 36 pp.

> Pp. v–vi, Introduction; text; 1–34, 35–6, Index.

(*b*) The Hastings' Journal of the Parliament of 1621. *Ed*. Lady de Villiers. R.H.S., 1953. xi, 46 pp.

> Pp. v–xi, Introduction; 1–34, text of Journal; 35–43, Appendix of correspondence (1623/4–1626); 45–6, Index.

(*c*) The Minute Book of James Courthope. *Ed*. Orlo Cyprian Williams. R.H.S., 1953. xv, 91 pp.

> Pp. v–xv, Introduction; 1–84, text of manuscript minute book kept by a Parliamentary committee clerk, 1697–9; 85–91, Index.

Volume LXXXIV

The Kalendar of Abbot Samson of Bury St. Edmunds and related documents. *Ed*. R. H. C. Davis. R.H.S., 1954. lx, 200 pp., frontispiece (map).

> P. vii, Foreword by V. H. Galbraith; ix–lvii, Introduction; lix, Note on transcription and editing; lx, List of abbreviations and references; 1–170, Latin texts; 171–95, Index of persons and places; 197–200, Index of subjects.

Volume LXXXV

The sermons of Thomas Brinton, bishop of Rochester, 1373–89. *Ed*. Sister Mary Aquinas Devlin. Vol. I. 1954. R.H.S. Pp. i–xxxviii, 1–240.

> Pp. v–vi, Preface; ix–xxxiv, Introduction; xxxv–xxxviii, List of sermons; 1–240, Latin texts of sermons 1–53, with explanatory headings in English.

Volume LXXXVI

The sermons of Thomas Brinton. ... Vol. II. R.H.S., 1954. Pp. i–v, 241–518.

> Continues C 252 *above*. Pp. 241–501, Latin texts of sermons 54–108; pp. 503–4, Appendix A, Will of Thomas de Brinton; pp. 505–11, Subject index; 513–8, Index of references.

Volume LXXXVII

The War of Saint-Sardos, 1323–5. Gascon correspondence and diplomatic documents. *Ed*. Pierre Chaplais. R.H.S., 1954. xxi, 302 pp. + *errata* slip.

> Pp. vii–xiii, Introduction; p. xiv, Correction; pp. xv–xxi, Table of documents; pp. 1–252, texts in Latin and French, with descriptive headings in English; 253–6, Appendix I, 'Opinions of English officials on the case of Saint-Sardos tried before the Parliament of Paris'; 257–66, Appendix II, 'English requests for restitution of lands occupied by the French and compensation for damages (1327)'; 267–70, Appendix III, 'Notes on Queen Isabella's itinerary in France, 9 March–14 November 1325'; 271–4, Appendix IV, 'List of English officials and captains of castles in Gascony, October 1323–November 1325'; 275–8, Appendix V, Supplementary documents; 279–302, Index of persons and places.

Volume LXXXVIII

Cartulary of the priory of St. Gregory, Canterbury. *Ed*. Audrey M. Woodcock. R.H.S., 1956. xxi, 209 pp.

> Pp. vii–xix, Introduction; p. xx, Note on transcription and editing; xxi, Abbreviations; 1–164, Latin texts, with descriptive headings in

English; 165–71, Appendix I, 'Related charters not included in the cartulary; 172–3, Appendix II, 'List of priors and officials'; 174–6, Appendix III, 'Sources for dating the inhabitants of Canterbury'; 177–180, Appendix IV, 'Distribution of the possessions of the priory'; 181–204, Index 1, Persons and places; 205–9, Index 2, Subjects.

Volume LXXXIX C 256

The chronicle of Walter of Guisborough, previously edited as the chronicle of Walter of Hemingford or Hemingburgh. *Ed.* Harry Rothwell. R.H.S., 1957. xlii, 409 pp. [Issued in respect of the years 1955–6 and 1956–7].

P. vii, Prefatory note; ix–x, List of abbreviations; xi–xlii, Introduction, including six Appendices; 1–398, Latin text; 399–409, Index.

Volume XC C 257

Camden Miscellany, Vol. XXI. R.H.S., 1958. In two sections separately paged, viz.

(*a*) The chronicle attributed to John of Wallingford. *Ed.* Richard Vaughan. R.H.S. 1958. xv, 74 pp.

P. vii, List of abbreviations; ix–xv, Introduction; 1–67, Latin text; 69–74, Index.

(*b*) A journal of events during the Gladstone Ministry, 1864–74. By John, first earl of Kimberley. *Ed.* Ethel Drus. R.H.S., 1958. xx, 49 pp.

P. iii, Prefatory note; vii–xx, Introduction; 1–44, text of Journal; 45–9, Index.

Volume XCI C 258

The Diurnal of Thomas Rugg, 1659–61. *Ed.* William L. Sachse. 1961. R.H.S., xxi, 203 pp.

Pp. i–xix, Preface and Introduction; xxi, Editorial note; 1–180, extract from 'Mercurius Politicus Redivivus . . . serveing as an Annuall Diurnall . . .'; 181–203, Index.

Volume XCII C 259

Liber Eliensis. Ed. E. O. Blake. R.H.S., 1962. lx, 463 pp.

Pp. ix–xviii, Foreword, by Dorothy Whitelock; xix–xxi, list of abbreviations; xxiii–lx, Introduction; 1–394, Latin text; 395–9, Appendix A, *Libellus quorundam insignium operum Beati Ædelwoldi episcopi*; 400–1, Appendix B, Extracts from the Book of Miracles in Brit. Mus. MS. Cotton, Domitian XV; 402–9, Appendix C, The litigation of Ely Cathedral priory (1150–69); 410–32, Appendix D, Some comments on

Book II of the *Liber Eliensis*; 433–6, Appendix E, The activities of Bishop Nigel of Ely between 1139 and 1144; 437, The *Passio* of St. Thomas Becket (note); 439–63, General index.

Volume XCIII C 260

The household papers of Henry Percy, ninth earl of Northumberland, 1564–1632. *Ed.* G. R. Batho. R.H.S., 1962. lvii, 190 pp. + four plates.

P. vii, Preface; xi–xv, Select bibliography; xvii–lvi, Introduction; lvii, Note on the editing of the manuscripts; 1–133, Texts, viz. 'Examples of accounting documents', 'The declarations of account for the audit period 1585–7', 'A selection of general accounts', 'Inventories, will and administration of will'; 135–46, Appendix I, 'A list of the summary accounts of the Northumberland household, 1585–1632'; 147, Appendix II, 'The Percy family pedigree'; 148–64, Appendix III, 'A list of the servants in the Percy household, 1585–1632'; 165–9, Appendix IV, 'A list of the creditors of the ninth earl of Northumberland, 1585–1632'; 171–5, Glossary; 177–90, Index.

Volume XCIV C 261

The parliamentary diary of Sir Edward Knatchbull, 1722–30. *Ed.* A. N. Newman. R.H.S., 1963. xiv, 162 pp., frontis. (portrait).

Pp. vii–xiv, Introduction; 1–114, text; 115–22, Appendix A, 'Samuel Sandys' memoranda'; 123, Appendix B, 'Extracts from the Finch manuscripts'; 124–30, Appendix C, 'Parliamentary reports from the Egmont manuscripts'; 131–51, Appendix D, 'Thomas Tower's memoranda'; 152–5, Appendix E, 'Comparative table of debates'; 156–62, Index.

ROYAL HISTORICAL SOCIETY

Camden series

FOURTH SERIES

Volume I

Camden Miscellany, Vol. XXII. R.H.S., 1964. v, 194 pp. In three sections, with Index, continuously paged, viz.

(*a*) Pp. 1–75, 'Charters of the earldom of Hereford, 1095–1201.' *Ed.* David Walker.

Pp. 1–11, Introduction; 12, List of abbreviations.

(*b*) Pp. 77–112, 'Indentures of retinue with John of Gaunt, Duke of Lancaster, enrolled in Chancery, 1367–99'. *Ed.* N. B. Lewis.

Pp. 77–85, Introduction; 86, List of retainers; 87–112, texts in French.

(*c*) Pp. 113–78, 'Autobiographical memoir of Joseph Jewell, 1763–1846'. *Ed.* Arthur Walter Slater.

Pp. 113–25, Introductory note on Jewell, 'one of the pioneers of the fine chemical industry in England'; 126–61, text of memoir; 162, Appendix A, Bibliography of printed works by Joseph Jewell; 163–5, Appendix B, 'Jewell's patent specification, A.D. 1807'; 166–78, Appendix C, 'Howard, Jewell and Gibson: financial arrangements and deed of co-partnership'.

Pp. 179–94, Index to whole volume.

Volume II

Documents illustrating the rule of Walter de Wenlok, abbot of Westminster, 1283–1307. *Ed.* Barbara F. Harvey. 1965. vii, 285 pp.

Pp. 1–45, Introduction, including 34–45, 'Wenlok's itinerary'; 47, Editorial note; 48, List of abbreviations; 49–248, texts of writs, accounts, compositions, household ordinances; 249–51, Glossary; 253–85, Index.

Volume III

The early correspondence of Richard Wood, 1831–41. *Ed.* A. B. Cunningham. R.H.S., 1966. v, 281 pp.

Pp. 1–39, Introduction; 41–276, text of correspondence chiefly between Wood in Syria and Lord Ponsonby, British Ambassador in Constantinople; 277, Glossary; 279–81, Index.

Volume IV   C 265

Letters from the English abbots to the chapter at Cîteaux, 1442–1521. *Ed.* C. H. Talbot. R.H.S., 1967. [v], 282 pp.

Pp. 1–15, Introduction; 17–269, transcripts in Latin, with explanatory headings to each letter; 271–82, Index.

CATALOGUES

A descriptive catalogue of the works of the Camden Society: CX 1 stating the nature of their principal contents, the periods of time to which they relate, the dates of their composition, their manuscript sources, authors, and editors. Accompanied by a classified arrangement and an index; and by some illustrative particulars that have arisen since their publication. By John Gough Nichols. Westminster: printed by and for J. B. Nichols & Sons, 1862. xvi, 72 pp.

Pp. iii–viii, Preface, 'The Camden Society'; ix–xiv, 'Classification of works arranged with regard to their chronology'; xv–xvi, 'Sources of the manuscripts printed'; 1–68, 'Descriptive catalogue of the works of the Camden Society' [including additional notes]; 69–72, Index.

A descriptive catalogue of the first series of the works of the   CX 2 Camden Society: stating the nature of their principal contents [etc., as in 1st edition] . . . their publication. By J. G. Nichols. 2nd edition Westminster: Nichols, 1872. xxi, 91 pp.

Pp. iii–ix, Preface, 'The Camden Society'; xi–xviii, Classification of works; xix–xxi, 'Sources of the manuscripts printed'; 1–86, 'Descriptive catalogue of the works of the Camden Society', old series, vols. 1–105; 87–91, Index.

Catalogue of the first series of the works of the Camden   CX 3 Society, in numerical order: together with the abbreviations of their titles used in the General Index. C.S., [1881]. Pp. 1–144.

Pp. 1–12, Catalogue; 13–14, Explanation of abbreviations; 14–144, General Index, A—Baudouin only. [The work, started by Henry Gough, was never completed. Bound into volume: Camden Society, Report of the Council, 1880–1 (4 pp.)].

TRANSACTIONS OF THE
ROYAL HISTORICAL SOCIETY

[OLD SERIES]

* First issued as *Transactions of the Historical Society of Great Britain*, Volume I, Part 1 (1871) and Volume I, Part 2 (1872). The statement quoted above from the Preface to the 2nd edition is inaccurate: see the Introduction to the present work, pp. vii–viii above.

historical illustrations. By Charles Rogers. [Includes text of *The Staggering state*, ed. Walter Goodal (1754), with amendments.]

430–6. An official inaccuracy respecting the death and burial of the Princess Mary, daughter of King James I. By Joseph Lemuel Chester.

437–43. Was the old English aristocracy destroyed by the Wars of the Roses? By T. L. Kington Oliphant.

444–8. Index.

Volume II (1873)* T 2

Preface: 'The present volume includes the more important papers read at the various meetings of the Society during session 1871–2, and a portion of those read during session 1872–3. . . .'

Pp. 5–8. Fellows of the Royal Historical Society.

9–14. Inaugural address. By Earl Russell, President.

15–31. Es-Sukhra, the locked-up stone of Jerusalem. By Sir Edward Cust.

32–53. Life and naval career of Admiral Sir Richard J. Strachan, baronet, G.C.B. By Thomas A. Wise.

54–76. Podiebrad. Bohemia past and present. By Professor de Vericour. [George of Podiebrad, King of Bohemia, 1448.]

77–93. Wat Tyler. By Professor de Vericour.

94–116. Notes in the history of Sir Jerome Alexander, Second Justice of the Court of Common Pleas and Founder of the Alexander Library, Trinity College, Dublin. By Charles Rogers. [Reprint of paper in *Transactions*, vol. I (1st edn.)]

117–41. Further notes in the history of Sir Jerome Alexander. By John P. Prendergast.

142–57. Materials for a domestic history of England. By George Harris.

158–98. Borrowings of modern from ancient poets. By Sir John Bowring.

199–211. Memorials of Dr. John Old, the reformer. By William Watkins Old.

212–21. History of the Trent bridges at Nottingham. By John Potter Briscoe.

222–96. An estimate of the Scottish nobility during the minority of James VI, and subsequently, with preliminary observations. By Charles Rogers.

297–392. The poetical remains of King James the First of Scotland, with a memoir, and an introduction to his poetry. By Charles Rogers. [With reproduction of portrait opp. p. 297.]

393–438. Domestic everyday life, manners and customs in the ancient world. By George Harris.

439–52. Notes in ethnography. By George Twemlow.

453–55. Appendix. Supplementary notes to the history of the Scottish house of Roger. By Charles Rogers. [See *Transactions*, vol. I, p. 239.]

Volume III (1874)* T 3

Pp. vii–xi. Fellows of the Royal Historical Society.

1–74. Domestic everyday life, manners and customs in the ancient world. By George Harris. [Continued from vol. II, p. 438.]

75–97. Old found lands in North America. By Thomas Morgan. [Voyages of Leif Ericson and others.]

98–162. The rise of the English legal profession. By J. W. Hill. [With four appendices of documents.]

163–294. Three poets of the Scottish Reformation: Alexander Cunningham, fifth earl of Glencairn; Henry Balnarves of Halhill; and John Davidson, minister at Prestonpans. By Charles Rogers. [With illustrations and copious quotations from poems.]

295–345. The great mace and other corporation insignia of the borough of Leicester. By William Kelly. [337–45, Appendix, 'Corporate emblems and insignia in England and Wales'.]

346–71. Adventures of a Bohemian nobleman in Palestine and Egypt in the days of Queen Elizabeth. By A. H. Wratislaw, [Christopher Harant of Polzitz.]

372–9. Notes in the history of British life assurance. By George Tomkins.

380–94. On the possibility of a strictly scientific treatment of universal history. By Gustavus George Zerffi.

395–407. Malta and its knights. By Samuel Cowdy.

408–20. The art revival in Italy. By George Browning. [During the renaissance.]

421–54. Some account of Sir Audley Mervyn, His Majesty's Prime Sergeant and Speaker in the House of Commons in Ireland, from 1661 till 1666. By John P. Prendergast. [Pp. 450–4, Mervyn genealogy.]

455–66. Index.

* Volume II (1873) and Volume III (1874) were described on their title pages as 'new series', but this mistake was thereafter discontinued.

Volume IV (1876) T 4

Pp. v–viii. List of Fellows.

1–74. Historical notices and charters of the priory of Beauly. By Edmund Chisholm-Batten. [With extracts concerning Valliscaulian house on Beauly Firth, Ross-shire.]

75–96. Immanuel Kant in his relation to modern history. By Gustavus George Zerffi.

97–187. The history of landholding in England. By Joseph Fisher. [General sketch to 1875.]

188–230. Orientations of ancient temples and places of worship. By Charles Warren. [In Egypt, Israel and adjacent countries.]

231–59. Historical notices of the cradle of Henry V. By William Watkins Old. [With illustrations.]

260–363. Memoir of George Wishart, the Scottish martyr. With his translation of the Helvetian Confession and a genealogical history of the family of Wishart. By Charles Rogers.

364–415. Domestic everyday life, manners and customs in the ancient world. By George Harris. [Continued from *Transactions*, Vol. III, p. 74.]

416–23. Historical notices of John Bunyan. By George Hurst.

424–38. Thomas Mulock: an historical sketch. By Elihu Rich. [Friend of George Canning.]

439–48. St. Procop of Bohemia: a legend of the eleventh century. By A. H. Wratislaw.

449–53. Index.

Volume V (1877) T 5

P. ix, Office bearers of the Royal Historical Society for 1876–7; xi–xvi, List of Fellows.

1–27. Some considerations on the origins of monarchical government. By G. Laurence Gomme. [From Old Testament and Greek times.]

28–82. John Foxe the martyrologist and his family. By William Winters. [Including extracts from correspondence and diaries.]

83–116. Domestic every-day life and manners and customs in this country from the earliest period to the end of the last century. By George Harris. [Entirely concerned with pre-Roman and Roman Britain.]

117–43. The historical development of idealism and realism.

By Gustavus George Zerffi. [From Plato and Aristotle to Darwin.]

144–72. The siege of Quebec. By Sydney Robjohns.

173–215. Passages in the life and reign of Harold, the last of the Saxon kings. By William Winters.

216–27. On the establishment of Swiss freedom and the Scandinavian origin of the legend of William Tell. By James Heywood.

228–326. The history of landholding in Ireland. By Joseph Fisher. [From earliest times to eighteenth century.]

327–38. History of the county of Cilly [in Styria, 1362–1457]. By A. H. Wratislaw.

339–53. On the phenomena of historical representation: a study of the relation of historical to scientific research. By Benjamin W. Richardson.

354–79. Rehearsal of events which occurred in the north of Scotland from 1635 to 1645 in relation to the National Covenant. Edited from a contemporary MS. by Charles Rogers.

380–412. Historical notices of, and documents relating to, the monastery of St. Anthony at Leith. By Charles Rogers.

413–23. Index. [424], *Errata*.

Volume VI (1877)   T 6

Pp. v–xi. Royal Historical Society: Office-bearers, List of Fellows, Corresponding Members and Honorary Members, Societies exchanging Transactions.

1–85. On the epoch of Hittite, Khita, Hamath, Canaanite, Lydian, Etruscan, Peruvian, Mexican, etc. By Hyde Clarke. [Relationships revealed by philological and place-name evidence; pp. 40–56, table giving 'Comparison of Canaanite town names'; 71–80, Appendix I, comparative names of rivers, lakes and towns; 81–5, Appendix II, 'Table of Sumerian words'.]

86–130. Domestic everyday life, and manners and customs in this country, from the earliest period to the end of the eighteenth century: II, From the coming of the Anglo-Saxons to the Norman Conquest. By George Harris. [Continued from *Transactions*, vol. V, p. 116.]

131–46. Sovereignty in relation to the origin of social institutions. By G. Laurence Gomme. [Including 'law and religion as formative agents of society'.]

147–82. The early intercourse of the Danes and Franks. By Henry H. Howorth.

Volume VII (1878) T 7

212–48. Early bills of mortality. By Cornelius Walford.

249–308. On the settlement of Britain and Russia by the English races. By Hyde Clarke. ['Warings', 'Rugians', etc.]

309–29. Some account of ancient churchwarden accounts of St. Michael's, Bath. By Charles Buchanan Pearson. [With extracts, from 1379.]

330–61. Historical notices of the family of Margaret of Logy, second queen of David the Second, King of Scots. By A. Stewart Allan.

362–83. The growth of nationality in Canada. By Sydney Robjohns.

384–94. Inaugural address of the Right Hon. Lord Aberdare, President of the Royal Historical Society. [The value of historical studies.]

395–444. The Columban clergy of North Britain and their harrying by the Norsemen. By Henry H. Howorth.

445–7. Index.

[Bound into volume: Report of the Council and Balance Sheet for year ending Oct. 31, 1878 (7 pp.). The report contains a brief statement of the Society's origin and progress.]

Volume VIII (1880)   T 8

Pp. vii–viii. Preface by Charles Rogers.

ix–xxiii. Lists of Fellows, Corresponding Members, Honorary Members, foreign associations which exchange Transactions with the Society, etc.

1–11. Notes on the study of history. By Charles Rogers.

12–19. Vladimir Monomachus, Grand Prince of Kyjev [d. 1125]. By Albert H. Wratislaw.

20–35. The origin of the office of Poet Laureate. By Walter Hamilton. [P. 35, 'Table of the Poets Laureate of England'.]

36–63. Domestic every-day life, manners and customs in this country, from the earliest period to the end of the eighteenth century. By George Harris. Part IV. From the end of the thirteenth to the commencement of the sixteenth century. [Pp. 62–3 give a reply, by Charles Rogers, to 'certain strictures which have been made on these papers'.]

64–69. The corporation of Bedford, an historical sketch. By George Hurst.

70–162. Early laws and customs in Great Britain regarding food. By Cornelius Walford. [From 1217 to 1844, largely extracted from author's *History of the famines of the world*.]

Volume IX (1881)   T 9

152–73. The reconstruction of the civilization of the West, from Charlemagne (*Transitio Imperii*) to the era of the Crusades (and Concordat, 1122). By W. J. Irons.

174–215. The early history of Sweden. By Henry H. Howorth.

216–23. Narrative of the transference of the German Weimarian army to the crown of France in the seventeenth century. By James Heywood.

224–53. Domestic everyday life, manners, and customs in this country ... Part V. From the commencement of the sixteenth century to the commencement of the eighteenth century. By George Harris.

254–67. Index. [Bound into volume: Report of Council, 1880–1 (8 pp.).]

Volume X (1882)   T 10

Pp. vii–xxviii, Officers, Council, Fellows, etc. (1882).

Pp. 1–74. Kings Briefs: their purposes and history. By C. Walford. [Issued for charitable purposes, 1206–1828. Appendix 1, 'Collections upon Briefs at Clent, Staffs., from 1672 to 1705'. Appendix 2, Examples from Corporation of London records, 1671–1716. Appendix 3, Other references, 1558–1815.]

75–81. Notes on the history of 'Old Japan' (Dai Nipon). By C. Pfoundes. [Abstract.]

82–92. Notes on the history of eastern adventure, exploration and discovery, and foreign intercourse with Japan. By C. Pfoundes. [Abstract.]

93–113. Notes from the Penrith registers. By Edward King. [Extracts, 1556–1687, with comments.]

114–33. On the history of theatres in London, from their first opening in 1576 to their closing in 1642. By F. G. Fleay. [Lists, pp. 131–3.]

134–202. The early history of the Mediterranean populations, etc., in their migrations and settlements, illustrated from autonomous coins, gems, inscriptions, etc. By Hyde Clarke. [With 'tables of cities, with their coins and emblems'.]

203–31. Domestic everyday life, manners and customs in this country ... Part VI. From the commencement to the termination of the eighteenth century. By George Harris.

232–47. The struggle of the Christian civilization from the era of the Crusades to the fall of the East (1453). By W. J. Irons.

248–66. On certain points of analogy between Jewish and Christian baptism in the apostolic age. By J. Baker Greene.

267–311. Notices of the Pilgrim Fathers. John Eliot and his friends, of Nazing. Collected from original sources. By William Winters. [With extracts.]

312–43. Abraham Lincoln. By Hon. Isaac N. Arnold.

344–70. Voltaire in his relation to the study of general history, from a philosophical point of view. By G. G. Zerffi.

371–77. Index.

[Bound into volume: Report of the Council, session 1880–1. (9 pp.).]

NEW SERIES

Volume I   (1884) [Apparently issued quarterly.]   T 11

Pp. 1–15. Officers and Council, March 1884, Lists of Fellows, Corresponding Members, Honorary Fellows.

15–16. Foreign associations exchanging Transactions.

1–17. History on the face of England. By Henry Elliot Malden. [Place-names, geographical factors, etc.]

18–61. The early intercourse of the Franks and Danes, Part III. By Henry H. Howorth. [Continued from *Transactions*, VII.]

62–9. Notes on the Ligurians, Aquitanians and Belgians. By Hyde Clarke.

70–83. The Iklîk, by Hamdâni. By G. G. Zerffi. [Tenth century historical poem about ancient Arab origins.]

84–92. Bibliographical notices. [First of quarterly series, dealing with British and foreign publications.]

93–118. The English acquisition and loss of Dunkirk. By S. A. Swaine.

119–32. Historical allusions in sundry English poets: I Chaucer, II Gascoigne. By F. G. Fleay.

133–57. The Emperor Frederick II of the house of Hohenstaufen. By Arthur Robert Pennington.

158–92. The Iberian and Belgian influence and epochs in Britain. By Hyde Clarke.

193–203. Bibliographical notices.

204–41. Political lessons of Chinese history. By Sir Richard Temple. [Folding map of China opposite p. 204; supplementary 'Note' by Sir Thomas Wade, pp. 229–41.]

242–59. Pestilences: their influence on the destiny of nations, as shown in the history of the Plague. By J. Foster Palmer.

260–72. Hungary under King Matthias Hunyady, surnamed 'Corvinus', 1458–90. By G. G. Zerffi.

273–87. Bibliographical notices.

288. Obituary notices: Wiliam Josiah Irons, Frederic de Peyster.

289–308. Personal traits of Mahratta Brahman princes. By Sir Richard Temple.

309–63. The conquest of Norway by the Ynglings. By Henry H. Howorth.

364–75. Bridges: their historical and literary associations. By Cornelius Walford. [Chiefly Roman and Italian.]

376–84. The Keltic church and English Christianity. By William Dawson.

385–408. Bibliographical notices.

409–34. Index.

Volume II (1885)   T 12

Pp. 1–60. Historical sketch of South Africa. By Sir Bartle Frere.

61–76. Notes on the local progress of Protestantism in England in the sixteenth and seventeenth centuries. By Henry Elliot Malden. [With references to map opposite p. 61.]

77–96. The Triple Alliance of 1788. By Oscar Browning.

97–112. Bibliographical notices.

113–15. Obituary notices: Joseph Drew (d. 1883), William Henley Jervis (d. 1884), John William Wallace (b. 1815).

117–72. Christianity in Roman Britain. By Henry H. Howorth.

173–96. The Saxon invasion and its influence on our character as a race. By J. Foster Palmer.

197–214. The language and literature of the English before the Conquest, and the effect on them of the Norman invasion. By Robinson Thornton.

215–23. Bibliographical notices.

225–53. The lost opportunities of the House of Austria. By G. B. Malleson.

254–71. The Tchōng-Yông of Confucius, edited by his grandson, Tchhing-Tsé. By G. G. Zerffi.

272–92. Historical suggestions in the ancient Hindu cpic, the Mahábhárata. By Charles J. Stone.

293–301. Origins of the New England Company, London, with an account of its labours on behalf of the North-American Indians. By William Marshall Venning.

302–34. The intercourse of the Danes with the Franks, etc. By Henry H. Howorth. [Continucd from T 11 p. 61.]

335–47. Bibliographical notices.

349–64. The treaty of commerce between England and France in 1786. By Oscar Browning.

365–89. Perplexities of oriental history. By Sir F. J. Goldsmid.

390–99. Bibliographical notices. By Gustave Masson.

401–13. Index.

[Bound into volume: Report of Council, 1883–4, lists of Officers, Council, Fellows, Corresponding Members, Honorary Fellows and Foreign Associations exchanging publications. (16 pp.).]

Volume III (1886)   T 13

Pp. 1–46. Examination of the legend of Atlantis in reference to protohistoric communication with America. By Hyde Clarke.

47–152. The story of Prince Henry of Monmouth and Chief-Justice Gascoign. By F. Solly-Flood.*

153–88. Obituary notice: Sir Bartle Frere. By Mary E. I. Frere.

189–203. Bibliographical notices. By Gustave Masson.

205–41. The imperial policy of Elizabeth from the State Papers, Foreign and Domestic. By Hubert Hall.

243–80. The Picts and pre-Celtic Britain. By Hyde Clarke.

281–91. Extracts from the Memoranda Rolls (L.T.R.) of the Exchequer. [Note on the negotiations preceding the *Confirmatio Cartarum* (1297 A.D.) and illustrative documents in Latin, with translations].

293–304. Obituary notices: Sir Bartle Frere, II. By Mary E. I. Frere. [Continued from p. 88.]

305–18. Bibliographical notices. By 'X' and Gustave Masson.

319–41. The flight of Louis XVI to Varennes: a criticism of Carlyle. By Oscar Browning.

343–70. The Celt in power: Tudor and Cromwell. By J. Foster Palmer [pp. 367–70, Appendix, pedigrees of Stuarts, Tudors, Cromwells, Plantagenet descent of Henry VIII].

371–92. The formation and decay of craft gilds. By William Cunningham.

393–406. Co-operative history. By A. R. Ropes.

407–22. Bibliographical notices.

423–4. Obituary notices: William Job Collins (d. 1884), W. Watkins Old (d. 1885).

425–38. Index.

[Bound into volume: Lists of Officers, Council, Fellows, etc. foreign associations exchanging publications. (16 pp.).]

---

* Reprinted with a few corrections and separately issued by Longmans Green in 1886.

Volume IV (1889) T 14

Pp. 1–40. Vercingetorix. By G. B. Malleson.

41–65. The historical connections of the Hittites. By C. R. Conder.

67–84. Conference on the teaching of history in schools. Held at the rooms of the Society of Arts, on Saturday, Oct. 22, 1887, Professor Mandell Creighton . . . in the chair. [Including, pp. 69–81, address on 'The teaching of history in schools', by Oscar Browning.]

85–101. Hugh Elliot in Berlin. By Oscar Browning. [Correcting Carlyle's story of the stealing of the papers of the American envoy, Arthur Lee, in 1777.]

103–23. Historic genealogy. By H. E. Malden.

125–41. Prince Henry of Monmouth—his letters and despatches during the war in Wales, 1402–5. By Frederick Solly Flood. [With quotations.]

143–70. The causes of the Seven Years' War. By Arthur R. Ropes.

171–96. Historical evidence and information gathered from the traders' tokens of the seventeenth century and from the minor currency. By George C. Williamson.

197–220. The commercial policy of Edward III. By W. Cunningham.

221–84. Historical sketch of South Africa. By Sir Bartle Frere. [Continued from T 12 p. 60. '*Unfinished MS.*'.]

285–302. History and assassination. By Herbert Haines.

303–48. The tradition of the Archaian white races. By J. S. Stuart Glennie.

349–50. Jubilee Address to Her Majesty the Queen [July 1887].

351. The Colonial Institute [Appeal for Imperial Institute fund.]

353–60. Bibliographical notices.

361–72. Index.

[Bound into volume: Lists of Officers, Council, Fellows, 1889 (16 pp.); Report of Council, 1886–7 (7 pp.); Report of Council, 1887–8 (5 pp.).]

Volume V (1891) T 15

Pp. 1–52. Babylonian chronology and history. By G. Bertin.

53–74. The sequence of forms of government in Plato's 'Republic', compared with the actual history of Greek cities. By H. E. Malden.

[Bound into volume: lists of Officers and Council (November 1891), Cambridge Branch Committee, Fellows, Foreign associations and libraries exchanging publications (16 pp.).]

Volume VI (1892)   T 16

[Introduction, transcript in Latin of the commission on inclosures, 28 May 1517, and tables arranged under counties.]

315–38. PRESIDENTIAL ADDRESS. By Sir Mountstuart E. Grant Duff. [On the study of history.]

339–53. The progress of historical research during the session 1891–2.

354–60. Index.

[Bound into volume: lists of Officers and Council, October 1892; Cambridge Branch, Committee; Fellows, foreign associations exchanging publications; libraries receiving Transactions (16 pp.); Report of Council, 1890–1 (7 pp.).]

Volume VII (1893)   T 17

Pp. 1–19. PRESIDENTIAL ADDRESS. By Sir Mountstuart E. Grant Duff. [Value of Thucydides to 'modern statesmen'.]

21–36. Notes on the family of Betoun in connection with some royal letters of James VI. By Henry Elliot Malden. [P. 34, Appendix A, Bethune family tree; pp. 35–6, Appendix B, extract, later than 1543, from charters and precepts of Clareconstat.]

37–53. The Magyar county: a study in the comparative history of municipal institutions. By Emil Reich.

55–75. The druids of Ireland. By Julius von Pflugk-Hartung. [Translated from the German.]

77–107. On the *Instituta Cnuti aliorumque regum Anglorum.* By F. Liebermann.

109–25. The laws of the Mercers Company of Lichfield. Communicated and transcribed from the original MS. by W. H. Russell, with an introduction by [W.] Cunningham. [Pp. 113–25 contain transcript, dated 1624.]

127–292. The inquisition of 1517. Inclosures and evictions. Edited from the Lansdowne MS. I. 153 by I. S. Leadam. Part II. [Continued from new ser. vol. VI (1892). Pp.127–33, Preface; 134–218, Norfolk: Introduction, tables, extracts and notes; 219 53, Yorkshire: Introduction, etc.; 254–69, Herefordshire: Introduction, etc.; 270–6, Staffordshire: Introduction, etc.; 277–92, Hampshire and the Isle of Wight: Introduction, etc.]

293–305. The progress of historical research during the session 1892–3.

307–23. Index.

[Bound into volume: Report of the Council, session 1891–2, lists of Fellows etc.]

Volume VIII (1894) T 18

Pp. 1–20. PRESIDENTIAL ADDRESS. By Sir Mountstuart E. Grant Duff. [Tacitus as a historian.]

21–48. The text of Henry I's coronation charter. By F. Liebermann. [With transcripts of Latin and Norman-French versions.]

49–70. Educational organization of the mendicant friars in England (Dominicans and Franciscans). By A. G. Little.

71–107. Antonio Perez in exile. By Martin A. S. Hume.

109–27. The colonial empire of the Portuguese to the death of Albuquerque. By C. Raymond Beazley.

129–55. The earldoms under Edward I. By T. F. Tout.

157–80. The case of Lucas and Lisle. By J. H. Round. [Execution of Sir Charles Lucas and Sir George Lisle in 1648.]

181–201. The principal causes of the renewal of the war between England and France in 1803. By Waldemar Ekedahl.

203–49. An account of the proceedings in Suffolk during the Peasants' Rising in 1381. By Edgar Powell. [Pp. 227–49, Appendix of documents.]

251–331. The inquisition of 1517. Inclosures and evictions. Edited from the Lansdowne MS. I. 153. By I. S. Leadam. Part III. [Continued from vol. VII (1893). Pp. 251–6, London and suburbs, Introduction, extracts and notes; 257–79, Berkshire, Introduction, etc.; 280–97, Gloucestershire, Introduction, etc.; 298–305, Cambridgeshire, Introduction, etc.; 306–31, Shropshire, Introduction, etc.]

333–59. Index.

[Bound in volume: Officers and Council, Nov. 1894, Committees, List of Fellows, etc. Report of the Council, session 1892–3.]

Volume IX (1895) T 19

Pp. 1–23. PRESIDENTIAL ADDRESS. By the Right Hon. Sir Mountstuart E. Grant Duff. [The value of Herodotus.]

25–9. A speech delivered by the Right Hon. Sir M. E. Grant Duff . . . chairman of the Gibbon Commemoration Meeting.

31–48. Address [at Gibbon Commemoration]. By Frederic Harrison.

49–73. The English *nouveaux-riches* in the fourteenth century. By Alice Law.

75–98. Alien merchants in England in the fifteenth century. By M. S. Giuseppi. [Appendix, 'Analysis of the returns of the subsidies on alien merchants granted 27 and 31 Henry VI'.]

99–117. The gild merchant of Shrewsbury. By W. Cunningham. [With texts of the two earliest rolls of members in the possession of the corporation, 1209–10 and 1219–20, pp. 105–117.]

119–65. Exploration under Elizabeth, 1558–1603. By C. Raymond Beazley.

167–88. The Tudors and the currency, 1526–60. By C. W. C. Oman.

189–213. The monetary movements of 1600–21 in Holland and Germany. By W. A. Shaw. [Appendix, German text of satirical song, *Kipper und Wipper* (1621) and translation, pp. 210–13.]

215–21. 'Walter of Henley'. By W. Cunningham. [Corrections and additions to his introduction to Miss Lamond's edition of *Walter of Henley*.]

223–70. Journey through England and Scotland made by Lupold von Wedel in the years 1584 and 1585. Translated from the original manuscript by Dr. Gottfried von Bülow, Superintendent of the royal archives in Stettin. [With an introductory note on the author.]

271–86. The progress of historical research. [Not only in Britain but in continental countries.]

287–96. Index.

[Bound into volume: Officers, Council, Fellows etc., 1895–6 (14 pp.); Report of Council 1893–4 (6 pp.).]

Volume X (1896)   T 20

Pp. 1–22. PRESIDENTIAL ADDRESS. By Sir Mountstuart E. Grant Duff. [On Aristotle's *Politics*.]

23–40. Shakespeare as a historian. By Henry Elliot Malden.

41–58. The Parliament of Lincoln, 1316. By Arthur Hughes.

59–83. Early colonial constitutions. By J. P. Wallis. [In the American colonies.]

85–109. Early Christian geography. By C. Raymond Beazley.

111–20. The foreign policy of William Pitt in the first decade of his ministry in its European significance. A review. Translated from the German of Felix Salomon.

121–54. Richard the Redeless. By S. H. D. Holton. [Rich. II.]

155–9. Index.

[Bound into volume: Report of the Council, session 1894–5, etc.]

Volume XI (1897) T 21

Pp. 1–17. PRESIDENTIAL ADDRESS. By Sir Mountstuart E. Grant Duff. [On Polybius.]

19–30. A proposal for a new historical bibliography. By Frederic Harrison. [Critical bibliography of English history.]

31–40. The *École des Chartes* and English records. By F. York Powell. [Plea for training of archivists in England.]

41–66. Some survivors of the Armada in Ireland. By Martin A. S. Hume.

67–87. Elizabethan village surveys. By W. J. Corbett. [With coloured map (opp. p. 70) based on two surveys, 1564 and 1586, of Horstead and Staninghall, Norfolk.]

89–112. On some political theories of the early Jesuits. By Neville Figgis.

113–31. A narrative of the pursuit of English refugees in Germany under Queen Mary. By I. S. Leadam. [Transcript from Exchequer Memoranda roll, with notes.]

133–8. The conference of Pillnitz [1791]. By Oscar Browning.

139–52. Goree: a lost possession of England. By Walter Frewen Lord.

153–8. Index.

159–212. Report of the Council, session 1895–6, etc.

Volume XII (1898) T 22

Pp. 1–16. PRESIDENTIAL ADDRESS. By Sir Mountstuart E. Grant Duff. [On Cicero and the modern statesman.]

17–79. Marston Moor. By C. H. Firth. [Facsimile of royal army's order of battle as frontispiece to volume. Pp. 69–79, Appendix of documents relating to the battle, 1644.]

81–93. The national study of naval history. By J. K. Laughton.

95–101. The national study of naval history. II, New methods of research. By Hubert Hall.

103–16. The meeting of the Duke of Marlborough and Charles XII at Altranstadt, April 1707. By A. E. Stamp. [With transcripts of letters from John Robinson.]

117–49. The sheriff's farm. By G. J. Turner. [Pp. 142–9, Appendix summarizing calculations of arms of counties and most important bailiwicks, 5 Hen. II–15 Hen. II.]

151–79. The Florentine wool traders in the middle ages. A bibliographical note. By Miss E. Dixon. [Pp. 173–8, lists of books containing material.]

181–224. A narrative of the journey of Cecilia, Princess of Sweden, to the court of Queen Elizabeth. By Margaret Morison. [Transcript from B.M. Royal MSS. and extracts from other documents.]

225–30. Index.

231–89. Report of the Council, session 1896–7, etc.

Volume XIII (1899) T 23

Pp. 1–16. PRESIDENTIAL ADDRESS. By Sir Mountstuart E. Grant Duff. [On the Abbé Dubois' writings on India.]

17–73. The raising of the Ironsides. By C. H. Firth. [Pp. 66–73, Appendices I–IV containing extracts from 'documents relating to this portion of Cromwell's career'.]

75–102. The fall of Cardinal Wolsey. By James Gairdner.

103–15. Politics at the Council of Constance. By J. Neville Figgis.

117–36. Pitt and Peel—1783–4, 1834–5. By Frank H. Hill. [Comparison of their parliamentary situations.]

137–98. Origin and early history of double monasteries. By Mary Bateson. [In Gaul, Ireland, England, Germany, Italy and Spain.]

199–247. The relations of the crown to trade under James I. (*Alexander Prize Essay* for 1898.) By F. Hermia Durham.

249–66. Index.

267–321. Report of the Council, session 1897–8, etc.

Volume XIV (1900) T 24

Pp. 1–18. PRESIDENTIAL ADDRESS. By A. W. Ward. [State of historical studies in England.]

19–52. The battle of Dunbar [1650]. By C. H. Firth. [Frontispiece of volume is plan of the battle by Payne Fisher. *Corrigenda*, p. 304.]

53–67. The alleged condemnation of King John by the court of France in 1202. By Kate Norgate.

69–121. The development of political parties during the reign of Queen Anne. (*Alexander Prize Essay* for 1899.) By Walter Frewen Lord.

123–41. The decay of villeinage in East Anglia. By Frances G. Davenport. [Illustrated from records of Forncett manor.]

143–74. Notes on the diplomatic correspondence between England and Russia in the first half of the eighteenth century. By Mrs. D'Arcy Collyer.

175–85. The oldest monument of Russian travel. By C. Raymond Beazley. [Account of his journey to the Holy Land by the Archimandrite Daniel of Kiev, *c.* 1106–7.]

187–230. The tribal hidage. By W. J. Corbett. [With coloured map opp. p. 202 showing districts of the hidage. Appendix, pp. 223–30, giving 'List of the hundreds in the hidated counties'.]

231–303. The inquisitions of depopulation in 1517 and the 'Domesday of Inclosures'. By Edwin F. Gay. [Criticizing communications of Leadam in new ser. vols. VI, VII and VIII.]

305–15. Index.

317–20. Report of the Council, session 1898–9.

321–72. Charter, bye laws, officers and Council, 1900–1, committees, lists of Fellows, etc.

Volume XV (1901)   T 25

Pp. 1–45. The later history of the Ironsides. By C. H. Firth.

47–130. The negotiations preceding the peace of Lunéville. By Miss L. M. Roberts. (*Alexander Prize Essay*, 1901). Pp. 121–30: Appendices I–V, transcripts of various documents; Appendix VI, 'Text of the Treaty of Lunéville', 9 Feb. 1801.]

131–50. The correspondence of an English diplomatic agent in Paris, 1669–77. By Miss M. B. Curran. [William Perwich.]

151–70. The advent of the Great Elector. By W. F. Reddaway. [Brandenburg under Frederick William, 1640–3. Pp. 160–4, Appendix I, Instructions to Joseph Avery, 23 Jan. 1641; 164–70, Appendix II, Avery to Secretary Edward Nicholas, 29 April 1642.]

171–247. The 'Denarius Sancti Petri' in England. By O. Jensen. [From Anglo-Saxon times. Pp. 190–247, Appendices of supporting documents.]

249–60. Index.

261–4. Report of the Council, session 1899–1900.

265–316. Royal Historical Society: information, charter, by-laws; officers and Council, 1901–2; standing committees; lists of Fellows, Honorary Fellows, corresponding members, subscribing libraries, societies exchanging publications, Transactions and publications of the Society.

Volume XVI (1902)   T 26

Pp. vii–xxv. PRESIDENTIAL ADDRESS. By G. W. Prothero. [Present state of historical studies in England.]

1–17. Some materials for a new edition of Polydore Vergil's 'History'. By Francis Aidan Gasquet.

19–67. The internal organization of the Merchant Adventurers of England. By W. E. Lingelbach.

69–96. The High Court of Admiralty in relation to national history, commerce and the colonization of America, A.D. 1550–1650. By R. G. Marsden.

97–132. The State Papers of the early Stuarts and the Interregnum. By Mrs. S. C. Lomas. [Pp. 131–2, Appendix listing material in Hist. MSS. Comm. Reports.]

133–58. An unknown conspiracy against King Henry VII. By I. S. Leadam. [Centred round Edmund de la Pole, Earl of Suffolk, in 1503. Pp. 152–8, transcript of Star Chamber Proceedings, H. VII, no. 24.]

159–200. The social condition of England during the Wars of the Roses. By Vincent B. Redstone. (*Alexander Prize Essay*, 1902.)

201–21. Index.

223–7. Report of the Council, session 1900–1.

229–96. Information, Officers and Council, 1902–3, Fellows, etc.

Volume XVII   (1903)   T 27

Pp. vii–xxxiv. PRESIDENTIAL ADDRESS. By G. W. Prothero. [Plea for a bibliography of British history.]

1–22. The English Premonstratensians. By F. A. Gasquet.

23–65. The intellectual influence of English monasticism between the tenth and the twelfth centuries. By Rose Graham. [*Alexander Prize Essay*, 1903.)

67–119. Royalist and Cromwellian armies in Flanders, 1657–62. By C. H. Firth. [Pp. 111–15, Appendix A, 'A True Accounte of the Officers of Dunkirke'; 115–16, Appendix B, Lockhart's letter to the Parliament, 31 Dec. 1659; 117–19, Appendix C, Notices of the fortifications of Dunkirk, 1661.]

121–73. The development of industry and commerce in Wales during the middle ages. By E. A. Lewis.

175–233. Italian bankers and the English crown. By Robert Jowitt Whitwell. [Pp. 218–20, Appendix A, Sources; 220–3, Appendix B, Transactions with English ecclesiastics; 224–9, Appendix C, Advances in the Court of Rome, 1219–33; 230, Appendix D, and 231–3, Appendix E, Latin transcripts from Chancery and Exchequer documents.]

61–77. Canning and the secret intelligence from Tilsit, July 16–23, 1807. By J. Holland Rose.

79–107. The northern policy of George I to 1718. By J. F. Chance.

109–32. The beginnings of the Anglo–Portuguese alliance. By Violet Shillington. [Especially the agreement of 1294 and Treaty of Windsor, 1386.]

133–47. The study of nineteenth-century history. By Percy Ashley. [Plea for study of Europe, and Britain in relation to it, since 1815.]

149–69. Sharp and the Restoration policy in Scotland. A study in the relations of church and state. By John Willcock. [James Sharp, Archbishop of St. Andrews.]

171–203. The Rebellion of the Earls, 1569. (*Alexander Prize Essay*.) By Rachel R. Reid. [Pp. 201–3, Appendix, 'The affair of the copper mine'.]

205–9. Index.

211–17. Report of the Council, session 1904–5.

THIRD SERIES

Volume I   (1907)   T 31

Pp. 1–17. PRESIDENTIAL ADDRESS. By William Hunt. [Contents include observations on: the Society's rooms and library, the deaths of Albert Sorel, Mary Bateson and F. W. Maitland, the Advanced Historical Teaching Fund in London, the founding of the Historical Association, the society's publications.]

19–31. On a contemporary drawing of the burning of Brighton in the time of Henry VIII. By James Gairdner.

33–97. The rise of Gaius Julius Caesar, with an account of his early friends, enemies and rivals. By Sir Henry H. Howorth.

99–137. The northern treaties of 1719–20. By J. F. Chance.

139–56. Some early Spanish historians. By James Fitzmaurice-Kelly.

157–79. The commercial relations of England and Portugal, 1487–1807. By Miss A. B. Wallis Chapman.

181–203. The diaries (home and foreign) of Sir Justinian Isham, 1704–36. By H. Isham Longden.

205–62. The minority of Henry III. Part II. By G. J. Turner. [Continued from *Transactions*, new ser. XVIII, 245.]

263–77. Some Elizabethan penances in the diocese of Ely. *Ed.* Hubert Hall. [Note and transcripts.]

279–97. Index.

299–301. Lists of Officers and Council, 1907–8, Committees.

302–13. Lists of Fellows, Hon. Fellows and Corresponding Members.

314–20. Libraries subscribing and societies exchanging publications.

Volume II (1908)   T 32

Pp. 1–19. PRESIDENTIAL ADDRESS. By William Hunt. [Including notes on MS. diary of Denys Scully while on deputation from Irish Catholics to Parliament, 1805. Frontispiece to volume is portrait of Scully.]

21–50. The ballad history of the reigns of Henry VII and Henry VIII. By C. H. Firth.

51–128. The rise of Gaius Julius Caesar, with an account of his early friends, enemies and rivals. By Sir Henry H. Howorth. Part II. [Continued from *Transactions*, 3rd ser. I, 33–97.]

129–51. The eclipse of the Yorkes. By Basil Williams. [The family of Philip Yorke, 1st Earl of Hardwicke.]

153–74. The diary of an Elizabethan gentlewoman. By Evelyn Fox. [With extracts from journal of Margaret, Lady Hoby, 1599–1605.]

175–87. The Bardon Papers. A collection of contemporary documents (MS. Eg. 2124) relating to the trial of Mary Queen of Scots, 1586. By Charles Cotton. [Pp. 184–7, Appendix: 'The contents of the Bardon Papers in the British Museum concerning Mary Queen of Scots and the Babington Conspiracy'.]

189–234. The siege of Madras in 1746 and the action of La Bourdonnais. By G. W. Forrest. [His acceptance of a bribe.]

235–67. The Peace of Paris, 1763. (*Alexander Prize Essay.*) By Kate Hotblack. [Pp. 260–3, Appendix A: The Bourbon alliance; 263–4, Appendix B: 'South American Trade' (transcript of B.M. MS.); 264–5, Appendix C: 'The galleons'; 265–6, Appendix D: The fisheries.]

269–72. Index.

273–94. Lists of Officers, Council, Fellows, etc. 1908–9.

Volume III (1909)   T 33

Pp. 1–21. PRESIDENTIAL ADDRESS. By William Hunt. [Contents include observations on: the Historical Association, the Advanced Historical Teaching (London) Fund, recent publications of Fellows and the Society, the Historical Congresses at Berlin and Saragossa, anniversaries, the progress of the Society.]

23–49. The bicentenary commemoration of William Pitt, first earl of Chatham (November 15, 1708–May 11, 1778). A report of the proceedings of the Royal Historical Society on the occasion of the above commemoration.

51–124. The ballad history of the reigns of the later Tudors. By C. H. Firth. [Appendix, pp. 119–24: text of *Newes from Flaunders . . . a new Ballad* (1600).]

125–95. Sir Otho de Grandison, 1238?–1328. By C. L. Kingsford. [With appendix of documents, pp. 188–95.]

197–236. The causes of the War of Jenkins' Ear, 1739. By H. W. V. Temperley.

237–53. English traders and the Spanish Canary inquisition in the Canaries during the reign of Queen Elizabeth. By Miss Leonora de Alberti and Miss A. B. Wallis Chapman.

255–69. The origin of the *Regium Donum*. By Clement E. Pike.

271–83. Index.

285–306. Royal Historical Society: lists of officers, council, etc.

Volume IV   (1910)   T 34

Pp. 1–20. PRESIDENTIAL ADDRESS. By W. Cunningham. [Chiefly on Gray's Inn and Lord Bacon.]

21–32. The finance of Lord Treasurer Godolphin. By I. S. Leadam.

33–45. The sources for the history of Sir Robert Walpole's financial administration. By Hubert Hall.

47–62. The two Sir John Fastolfs. By L. W. Vernon Harcourt. [Sir John of Caistor or Sir John of Nacton?]

63–81. Concerning the Historical Manuscripts Commission. By R. A. Roberts.

83–115. The Duc de Choiseul and the invasion of England, 1768–70. By Margaret Cotter Morison. [Appendices I–IV, texts of documents, pp. 107–15.]

117–39. The estate book of Henry de Bray of Harlestone, Northamptonshire, 1289–1340. By Miss Dorothy Willis.

141–62. The collection of ship-money in the reign of Charles

I. By Miss M. D. Gordon. [With appendices of tables from Audit Office Declared Accounts, etc., pp. 154–62.]

163–74. Index.

175–81. Report of the Council, Session 1908–09.

Volume V (1911)   T 35

Pp. 1–20. PRESIDENTIAL ADDRESS. By the Ven. Archdeacon William Cunningham. [Principally on national institutions in England and Scotland, including the game of golf.]

21–61. The ballad history of the reign of James I. By C. H. Firth.

63–88. Respublica Christiana. By J. Neville Figgis. ['The concession theory' of the Church within the State and the challenge to it.]

89–103. The intrigue to deprive the earl of Essex of the Lord Lieutenancy of Ireland. By Clement E. Pike.

105–40. Notes on the Agincourt Roll. By J. Hamilton Wylie.

141–56. The possession of Cardigan Priory by Chertsey Abbey. A study in some mediaeval forgeries. By H. E. Malden.

157–91. The relations between England and the northern powers, 1689–97. Part I—Denmark. By Miss M. Lane. [Appendix 'Bibliography for the position of England towards the Northern Powers, 1689–97'.]

193–208. Some aspects of early English apprenticeship. By Miss O. Jocelyn Dunlop. [Sixteenth century.]

209–23. Index.

225–53. Report of the Council, 1909–10, etc.

Volume VI (1912)   T 36

Pp. 1–17. PRESIDENTIAL ADDRESS. By W. Cunningham. The family as a political unit [in Scotland and England].

19–64. The reign of Charles I. By C. H. Firth.

65–88. Some aspects of Castlereagh's foreign policy. By C.K. Webster.

89–128. The parish clergy of the thirteenth and fourteenth centuries. (*Alexander Prize Essay.*) By H. G. Richardson. [Pp. 120–3, Appendix I, The parish clergy and marriage; 124–5, Appendix II, The education of the parish clergy; 126–8, Appendix III, List of authorities quoted.]

129–62. The Commonwealth charters. By B. L. K. Henderson. [Pp. 155–62, Appendix 'A list of towns that applied for, or received, charters and grants under the Protectorate'.]

107

163–84. The Eastland Company in Prussia, 1579–85. By Adam Szelagowski and N. S. B. Gras.

185–220. The records of the English African companies. By Hilary Jenkinson. [The Company of Royal Adventurers of England trading into Africa, the Royal African Company, and the Company of Merchants trading to Africa. P. 218, page of register giving career of Richard Miles (1765–82); 219–20, transcript of letter, dated 22 Feb. 1787, from Sarah O'Keefe to her husband Daniel.]

221–31. Index.

233–61. Report of the Council, session 1910–11, etc.

Volume VII (1913) T 37

Pp. 1–24. PRESIDENTIAL ADDRESS. The guildry and trade incorporations in Scottish towns. By W. Cunningham. Including 'Sidelights on English conditions'. Pp. 16–24, Appendix, 'Architectural design' in Scotland and England].

25–48. The development of the study of seventeenth-century history. By C. H. Firth.

49–101. England and the Polish–Saxon problem at the Congress of Vienna. By C. K. Webster. [Pp. 70–101, Appendix, transcripts from P.R.O., 'F.O. Continent' series 6–11, 27 Nov. 1814–16 Feb. 1815.]

103–28. Castlereagh's instructions for the conferences at Vienna, 1822. By J. E. S. Green. [Proposed meetings transferred to Verona.]

129–50. The pedigree of Earl Godwin. By Alfred Anscombe. [P. 150, Pedigree showing 'the descent of Earl Godwin'.]

151–66. Some mercenaries of Henry of Lancaster, 1327–30. By V. B. Redstone. [Pp. 165–6, Appendix A, transcript of letter in French from Aldermen of Bury St. Edmunds to Lord Mayor, Aldermen, etc. of London, 1328; 166, Appendix B, transcript of letter in French from Henry of Lancaster to Lord Mayor, etc. of London, 5 Nov. 1328.]

167–89. Side-lights upon the assessment and collection of the mediaeval subsidies. By James F. Willard.

191–208. The Order of the Holy Cross (Crutched Friars) in England. By Egerton Beck.

209–19. Index.

221–61. Report of the Council, session 1911–12, etc.

Volume VIII (1914) T 38

Pp. 1–16 PRESIDENTIAL ADDRESS. By C. H. Firth. [*Desiderata* for seventeenth-century British history.]

17–39. The authenticity of the 'Lords' Journals' in the sixteenth century. By A. F. Pollard. [Pp. 38–9, 'Note on the Clerks of the Parliaments, 1485–1642'.]

41–54. The forthcoming bibliography of British history. By Henry R. Tedder.

55–76. John Wycliffe, the reformer, and Canterbury Hall, Oxford. By H. S. Cronin. [Dealing with contest between regulars and seculars and suggesting Wycliffe was secular Warden.]

77–102. Mounted infantry in mediaeval warfare. By J. E. Morris. [English examples; p. 96, 'Comparative table of county levies', 1322, 1337–8 and 1338.]

103–11. Prégent de Bidoux's raid in Sussex in 1514 and the Cotton MS. Augustus I (*i*), 18. By Alfred Anscombe. [With reference to the paper by J. Gairdner in *Transactions*, 3rd ser. I (1907) and the frontispiece map in that volume. *See* T 31.]

113–17. Secular aid for excommunication. By R. C. Fowler. [Cases from 1216 to 1565 in Chancery 'Significations of excommunication'.]

119–59. Manuscripts at Oxford relating to the later Tudors, 1547–1603. By F. J. Routledge. [Examples from Ashmole, Tanner, Rawlinson, Carte, Douce, Dodsworth, Perrott and other MSS. in Bodleian Library. Pp. 157–8, Appendix I, Transcript of letter from Princess Elizabeth to Protector Somerset, 6 Feb. 1548–9; 158, Appendix II, transcript of Leicester to North, 2 Aug. 1584; 159, Appendix III, Leicester to [?] North, 13 Dec. [year?].]

161–70. Index.

171–233. Report of the Council, session 1912–13, etc.

Volume IX (1915) T 39

Pp. 1–20. PRESIDENTIAL ADDRESS. By C. H. Firth. [English and British policy towards the Netherlands from middle ages to 1914.]

21–64. The Despenser War in Glamorgan [1321]. By J. Conway Davies.

65–76. A provincial assembly during the League. By Maurice Wilkinson. [Meeting of Estates loyal to crown at Semur, May 1590. Folded-in transcript from Archives Dép. de Dijon (1564) opp. p. 71.]

77–93. The errors of Lord Macaulay in his estimation of the squires and parsons of the seventeenth century. By P. H. Ditchfield.

95–109. Municipal administration in the Spanish dominions in America. By F. A. Kirkpatrick.

111–22. A suggestion for the publication of the correspondence of Queen Elizabeth with the Russian Czars. By Inna Lubimenko.

123–65. The historical side of the Old English poem of 'Widsith'. By Alfred Anscombe. [Including suggested corrections to text published by R. W. Chambers in 1912 and Dr. Chambers's reply (pp. 156–62).]

167–74. The history of the Canadian archives. By A. G. Doughty. [P. 167, prefatory note by C. H. Firth.]

175–8. Index.

179–242. Report of the Council, session 1913–14, etc.

Volume X (1916)   T 40

Pp. 1–24. PRESIDENTIAL ADDRESS. The study of English foreign policy. By C. H. Firth.

25–50. Germany in the time of George I. By J. F. Chance.

51–76. Germany and the French Revolution. By G. P. Gooch.

77–114. The influence of the writings of Sir John Fortescue. By Caroline A. J. Skeel.

115–58. The sources available for the study of medieval economic history. By E. Lipson. [Footnote to p. 115: 'In this paper I am chiefly concerned with the economic history of English towns'.]

159–65. An unedited Cely letter of 1482. By Henry Elliot Malden. [Text appended.]

167–73. The burning of Brighton by the French. By L. G. Carr Laughton. [Suggesting 1545 as date.]

175–76. Index.

177–240. Report of the Council, Session 1914–15, etc.

Volume XI (1917)   T 41

Pp. 1–34. PRESIDENTIAL ADDRESS. England and Austria. By C. H. Firth. [Chiefly from seventeenth to nineteenth century.]

35–60. The mission of M. Thiers to the neutral powers in 1870. By J. Holland Rose.

61–85. The India Board, 1784–1858. By William Foster.

87–123. The treason legislation of Henry VIII, 1531–4. (*Alexander Prize Essay.*) By Isobel D. Thornley.

125–42. The Derwentwater Plot, 1663. By Henry Gee. [By Anabaptists and other dissenters.]

143–64. Charles V and the discovery of Canada. By H. P. Biggar. [Opposition to French activities from 1540.]

165–84. Duelling and militarism. By A. Forbes Sieveking. [P. 184, Appendix on Roman challenges.]

185–97. The historical manuscripts at Lambeth. By Claude Jenkins.

199–213. Index.

215–78. Report of the Council, session 1915–16, etc.

FOURTH SERIES

Volume I (1918)   T 42

Pp. 1–27. PRESIDENTIAL ADDRESS. By C. W. C. Oman. [Rumours and legends during wars from ancient times to 1918.]

28–58. Traces of primitive agricultural organization as suggested by a survey of the manor of Martham, Norfolk, 1101–1292. By W. Hudson. [Appendix containing lists of tenements, pp. 55–8.]

59–76. Wellington, Boislecomte and the Congress of Verona, 1822. By J. E. S. Green.

77–91. The correspondence of the first Stuarts with the first Romanovs. By Madame Inna Lubimenko. [Early seventeenth century.]

92–128. The Ceylon expedition of 1803. By Miss V. M. Methley.

129–56. The establishment of the great farm of the English customs. By A. P. Newton.

157–89. The place of the Council in the fifteenth century. (*Alexander Prize Essay.*) By T. F. T. Plucknett.

190–217. The system of British colonial administration of the crown colonies in the seventeenth and eighteenth centuries compared with the system prevailing in the nineteenth century. By H. E. Egerton.

218–35. The constitutional development of South Africa. By L. S. Amery.

236–53. The constitutional development of Canada. By E. M. Wrong.

255–66. Index.
267–301. Report of the Council, session 1916–17, etc.

Volume II (1919)   T 43

Pp. 1–19. PRESIDENTIAL ADDRESS. National boundaries and treaties of peace. By C. W. C. Oman. [From 1803.]

20–58. British and allied archives during the War. ['England' (pp. 20–23), by H. Hall; 'Scotland' (pp. 23–6), by R. K. Hannay; 'Ireland' (pp. 26–32), by H. Wood; 'Wales' (pp. 33–7), by John Ballinger; 'United States of America' (pp. 37–40), by J. Franklin Jameson; 'Italy' (pp. 41–7), by Emilio Re; 'Italy: the Vatican archives' (pp. 47–58), by F. A. Gasquet.]

59–93. The metropolitan visitation of the diocese of Worcester by Archbishop Winchelsey in 1301. By Rose Graham.

94–112. The relations of Henry Cardinal York with the British government. By Walter W. Seton. [Pp. 111–12, Appendix 'Summary of principal documents relating to the pension of Henry, Cardinal York'.]

113–31. The Whigs and the Peninsular War, 1808–14. By Godfrey Davies.

132–49. Science in the history of civilization. By Sir R. A. Gregory.

150–71. The question of the Netherlands in 1829–30. By G. W. T. Omond.

172–87. The trial of Sir Walter Raleigh. By Sir Harry L. Stephen. [Lecture delivered in connection with The Raleigh Tercentenary Commemoration.]

188–98. Index.
199–247. Report of the Council, session 1917–18, etc.

Volume III (1920)   T 44

Pp. 1–24. PRESIDENTIAL ADDRESS. East and West. By Sir C. W. C. Oman. [Conflicts with Middle East to 1517.]

25–51. British and allied archives during the war. Series II. By H. Hall and others. ['France' (pp. 27–8), by Ch. V. Langlois and C. Bémont; 'Belgium' (pp. 28–39), by J. Cuvelier; 'Canadian war records' (pp. 39–41), by H. P. Biggar; 'Australia's records of the war' (pp. 41–7), by the Secretary of the Dept. of Defence; 'Union of South Africa' (pp. 47–51), by C. Graham Botha.]

52–71. The voyage of Pedro Teixeira on the Amazon from Pará to Quito and back, 1637–9. By G. Edmundson.

72–102. The English in Russia during the second half of the sixteenth century. By Mildred Wretts-Smith.

103–14. Unpublished documents relating to town life in Coventry. By Miss M. Dormer Harris. [With extracts from royal and other letters, chiefly of sixteenth century, and quotations from the mayor, Robert Beake's diary 1655.]

115–35. The Black Death in Wales. By William Rees.

136–70. The Commons' Journals of the Tudor period. (*Alexander Prize Essay.*) By J. E. Neale.

171–80. Index.

181–229. Report of the Council, session 1918–19, etc.

Volume IV (1921)   T 45

Pp. 1–22. PRESIDENTIAL ADDRESS. Some mediaeval conceptions of ancient history. By Sir C. W. C. Oman.

23–48. Status of 'villani' and other tenants in Danish East Anglia in pre-Conquest times. By W. Hudson.

49–61. Family-, Court- and State-Archives (Haus-, Hof-, und Staats-Archiv) at Vienna. By Joseph Redlich.

62–80. The Council of the West. By Caroline A. J. Skeel.

81–102. Illustrations of the mediaeval municipal history of London from the Guildhall records. By A. H. Thomas.

103–39. Notes from the ecclesiastical court records at Somerset House. By Francis W. X. Fincham. [Including extracts, chiefly from records of Consistory Court of London.]

140–72. The extent of the English forest in the thirteenth century. By Margaret Ley Bazeley. [Folding sketch map showing extent of royal forest opp. p. 140; pp. 160–3, Appendix I 'List of royal forests in the middle of the thirteenth century' (Sketch map of Northamptonshire forests opp. p. 160); 164–5, Appendix II, Authorities used; 166–72, Appendix III, List of extant perambulations and inquisitions as to metes and bounds.]

173–210. The Norse settlements in the British Isles. By Alexander Bugge.

211–17. Index.

219–57. Report of the Council, session 1919–20, lists of officers etc.

Volume V (1922)   T 46

Pp. 1–27. The embassy of William Harborne to Constantinople, 1583–8. By H. G. Rawlinson.

113

Russian market in the seventeenth century. By Madame Inna Lubimenko.

52–76. The courts and court rolls of St. Albans Abbey. By Miss A. E. Levett.

77–97. Some aspects of medieval travel, notably transport and accommodation, with special reference to the wardrobe accounts of Henry, earl of Derby, 1390–3. (*Alexander Prize Essay.*) By Grace Stretton.

98–130. The English province of the order of Cluny in the fifteenth century. By Rose Graham. [Appendix I, 'The Cluniac houses in England and Wales' (pp. 127–8); Appendix II, 'Counties of England and Wales in which Cluniac houses were situated' (pp. 129–30).]

131–65. A reply to Mr. F. W. Buckler's 'The political theory of the Indian Mutiny'. By Douglas Dewar and H. L. Garrett. [Referring to article in *Transactions*, 4th ser. V (1922) 71–100. With F. W. Buckler's 'reply', pp. 160–5.]

167–73. Index.

175–215. Report of the Council, session 1922–3, etc.

Volume VIII (1925)   T 49

Pp. 1–13. PRESIDENTIAL ADDRESS. By J. W. Fortescue. [The human element in historical research.]

14–37. William IV of Orange and his English marriage. By P. Geyl. [To Princess Ann, eldest daughter of George II, in 1733.]

38–55. Debates in the House of Lords, 1628. By Frances H. Relf. [On the notes by Henry Elsing, Clerk of the Parliaments.]

56–78. Financial administration under Henry I. By Geoffrey H. White.

79–97. Coal-mining in the seventeenth century. By Asta Moller.

98–126. Devonshire ports in the fourteenth and fifteenth centuries. (*Alexander Prize Essay.*) By Frances A. Mace. [Pp. 124–6, Appendix: 'Foreign trade. Cargoes entering and leaving Devonshire ports.']

127–50. The beginning of the Dissolution: Christchurch, Aldgate, 1532. By Eliza Jeffries Davis. [House of Austin canons. Pp. 147–8, Appendix I, 'Extant surveys of the property of Christchurch'; 148–50, Appendix II, 'The aldermanry and portsoken' (transcripts of two documents, one dated 1544).]

151–70. Experiments in Exchequer procedure, 1200–32. By Mabel H. Mills.

171–90. The Exchequer year. By H. G. Richardson. [Variations in medieval practice of dating.]

191–203. Index.

205–45. Report of the Council, session 1923–4, etc.

Volume IX   (1926)   T 50

Pp. 1–28. PRESIDENTIAL ADDRESS. By T. F. Tout. [The history of the Royal Historical Society since 1868.]

29–62. Irish parliaments in the reign of Edward II. By Maude V. Clarke. [P. 57, Appendix I, 'List of Irish parliamenta in Edward II's reign'; 58–9, Appendix II, 'Sub-tenants summoned to the Parliament of Kilkenny in 1310'; 60–1, Appendix III, 'Bishoprics *inter Anglicos* from 1303–88'; 61–2, Appendix IV, 'Sources of Irish revenue under Edward II'.]

63–83. An episode in Anglo-Russian relations during the War of the Austrian Succession. By Sir Richard Lodge. [Quarrel between Friedrich Lorentz, or Frederick Laurence, British chargé at Berlin, and Voronzov, Russian Vice-Chancellor, in 1746.]

85–106. The authorship of the *Defensor Pacis*. (*Alexander Prize Essay*, 1926.) By Marian J. Tooley. [Marsilio of Padua and John of Jandun joint authors.]

107–34. The making of a crown colony: British Guiana, 1803–33. By Lillian M. Penson.

135–58. The cattle trade between Wales and England from the fifteenth to the nineteenth centuries. By Caroline Skeel. [Pp. 156–7, Appendix I, Transcript of account, from Wynn Papers, 12 Sept. 1670; 157–8, Appendix II, 'Some references to drovers in Welsh poems'.]

159–73. The foundations of English history. By F. M. Stenton. [Revision of early English history suggested by archaeological and other new evidence.]

175–6. The Exchequer year. *A supplementary note.* By H. G. Richardson. [With reference to his article in *Transactions*, 4th ser. VIII p. 171.]

177–88. Index.

189–229. Report of the Council, session 1924–5, etc.

Volume X   (1927)   T 51

Pp. 1–19. PRESIDENTIAL ADDRESS. National and international co-operation in historical scholarship. By T. F. Tout.

[With special reference to the International Committee of Historical Sciences.]

21–53. The reign of Henry III: some suggestions. By E. F. Jacob. [Pp. 48–53, Appendix: 'Memoranda of proceedings in Parliament, Edward I' (transcript in Latin).]

55–85. Illustrations of English history in the mediaeval registers of the parlement of Paris. By H. G. Richardson. [Facsimile of letter from Henry VI to parlement opp. p. 68. Pp. 78–85, Appendix: 'Note on the records of the parlement of Paris'.]

87–109. The diplomatic service under William III. By Miss M. Lane. [Pp. 107–9, Appendix: List of diplomatic representatives of England in Europe during the reign of William III.]

111–33. The reforms at the Exchequer, 1232–1242. By Miss M. H. Mills.

135–69. The Duchy of Cornwall: its history and administration, 1640 to 1660. By Mary Coate.

171–94. Some attempt at imperial co-operation during the reign of Queen Anne. By W. T. Morgan. [I.e., in American and West Indian colonies.]

195–263. The general and provincial chapters of the English Black Monks, 1215–1540. (*Alexander Prize Essay.*) By W. A. Pantin. [Pp. 245–56, Appendix A, 'List of general or provincial chapters and presidents'; 257, Appendix B, 'Manuscripts of the statutes of the York province'; 258, Appendix C, 'MS. collections of chapter documents, 1336–63'; 259–61, Appendix D, 'List of diffinitors'; 261–3, Appendix E, 'Attendances at general and provincial chapters'.]

265–85. Index. 287–344. Report of Council, 1925–6, etc.

Volume XI (1928)   T 52

Pp. 1–16. PRESIDENTIAL ADDRESS. The human side of mediaeval records. By T. F. Tout.

17–37. The Public Record Office and the historical student—a retrospect. By A. E. Stamp.

39–59. Anglo-Russian relations during the first English Revolution. By Ina Lubimenko.

61–82. The Merchant Adventurers of Bristol in the fifteenth century. By Eleanora M. Carus-Wilson.

83–115. A study in the history of Clare, Suffolk, with special reference to its development as a borough. (*Alexander Prize Essay,* 1928.) By Gladys A. Thornton. [Pp. 112–15, Appendix: List of 'Lords of the manor and borough of Clare' to 1553.]

117–36. The will of Polydore Vergil. By E. A. Whitney and P. P. Cram. [Pp. 131–6, Appendix: transcript of *Examinatum et registratum domino Polydoro viventi*.]

137–83. The origins of Parliament. By H. G. Richardson. [Pp. 172–5, Appendix I, 'Provisional list of English parliaments, 1258–72'; 176–83, Appendix II, 'The parlement of Alfonse of Poitiers at Toulouse in 1270': note and extracts in Latin from roll in Archives Nationales, headed *Arresta facta apud Tholosam anno domini millesimo ducentesimo septuagesimo*].

185–95. Index.

197–239. Report of the Council, session 1926–7, etc.

Volume XII (1929)   T 53

Pp. 1–17. PRESIDENTIAL ADDRESS. History and historians in America. By T. F. Tout.

19–48. The transformation of the Keepers of the Peace into the Justices of the Peace, 1327–80. By Bertha Haven Putnam.

49–74. The administration of the diocese of Ely during the vacancies of the see, 1298–9 and 1302–3. By Rose Graham.

75–104. The system of account in the Wardrobe of Edward II. By J. H. Johnson.

105–35. The imprisonment of Lord Danby in the Tower, 1679–84. By Miss A. M. Evans.

137–62. The relations of William III with the Swiss Protestants, 1689–97. By L. A. Robertson.

163–92. Lord Palmerston's policy for the rejuvenation of Turkey, 1839–41. (*Alexander Prize Essay*.) By F. S. Rodkey.

193–202. Index.

203–47. Report of the Council, session 1927–8, etc.

Volume XIII (1930)   T 54

Pp. 1–16. PRESIDENTIAL ADDRESS. Machiavelli's *Il Principe*. By Sir Richard Lodge.

17–49. The Public Records of Ireland before and after 1922. By Herbert Wood.

51–82. King Stephen's earldoms. By Geoffrey H. White.

83–116. School life in mediaeval Finland—mainly in the town of Viborg, illustrated by royal letters and local records. By Donald Smith. [Chiefly concerned with changes brought by Reformation, sixteenth to seventeenth centuries.]

117–47. The Spanish resistance to the English occupation of Jamaica, 1655–60. By Irene A. Wright.

149–85. The proposed Anglo-Franco-American treaty of 1852 to guarantee Cuba to Spain. (*Alexander Prize Essay.*) By A. A. Ettinger.

187–203. The later history and administration of the Customs revenue in England, 1617–1814. By B. R. Leftwich.

205–28. William Huskisson and the controverted elections at Liskeard in 1802 and 1804. By G. S. Veitch.

229–39. Index.

241–87. Report of the Council, session 1928–9, etc.

Volume XIV (1931)   T 55

Pp. 1–38. PRESIDENTIAL ADDRESS. The mission of Henry Legge to Berlin, 1748. By Sir Richard Lodge. [With 'Additional notes', summarizing references in *Politische Correspondenz Friedrichs des Grossen*, pp. 30–3].

39–63. Materials for the reign of Alfonso X of Castile, 1252–1284. By Evelyn S. Procter. [With Appendix, listing 'Unpublished documentary material', 'Published materials' and 'Modern books and articles', pp. 59–63.]

65–94. Forfeitures and treason in 1388. By Miss M. V. Clarke. [Inventories in the *Book of forfeitures* and other sources, proceedings of the Merciless Parliament.]

95–120. The borough business of a Suffolk town (Orford), 1559–1660. By R. A. Roberts.

121–40. English architecture in the seventeenth and eighteenth centuries. By Sir Reginald Blomfield.

141–73. English neutrality in the War of the Polish Succession. A commentary upon *Diplomatic instructions,* vol. VI, *France, 1727–44.* By Sir Richard Lodge.

175–96. The Elibank Plot, 1752–3. By Sir Charles Petrie.

197–224. The humanitarian movement of the early nineteenth century to remedy abuses on emigrant vessels to America. (*Alexander Prize Essay.*) By Miss K. A. Walpole.

225–49. Economic aspects of the negotiations of Ryswick. By W. T. Morgan.

251–66. Index.

267–314. Report of the Council, session 1929–30, etc.

Volume XV (1932)   T 56

Pp. 1–43. PRESIDENTIAL ADDRESS. Sir Benjamin Keene, K.B. A study in Anglo-Spanish relations in the earlier part of the eighteenth century. By Sir Richard Lodge.

45–90. William of Ely, the King's Treasurer, ?1195–1215. By H. G. Richardson. [With 'Appendix of illustrative documents', pp. 79–90.]

91–131. Wilkins's *Concilia* and the fifteenth century. By E. F. Jacob.

133–61. Edmund Dudley, minister of Henry VII. (*Alexander Prize Essay*.) By Miss D. M. Brodie.

163–79. Queen Elizabeth and the siege of Rouen. By R. B. Wernham.

181–210. The transference of lands in England, 1640–60. By H. Egerton Chesney.

211–42. The secret service under Charles II and James II. By James Walker. [Appendix I, 'Accompt' for intelligence, 1660–2; Appendix II, 'Bibliography', pp. 236–42.]

243–69. The Polwarth Papers. A commentary upon the Historical Manuscripts Commission Report, 1911–31. By Sir Richard Lodge.

271–88. Index.

289–334. Report of the Council, session 1930–1, etc.

Volume XVI (1933)   T 57

Pp. 1–43. PRESIDENTIAL ADDRESS. The Treaty of Seville (1729). By Sir Richard Lodge.

45–53. A discussion on the modern methods for the study of medieval history and their requirements. Modern methods of medieval research. By F. M. Powicke.

55–68. A discussion on the exploration of Anglo-American archives. Opened by Hubert Hall.

69–94. Bede as a classical and a patristic scholar. By M. L. W. Laistner.

95–128. Ranulf Flambard and early Anglo-Norman administration. (*Alexander Prize Essay*.) By R. W. Southern.

129–60. Woburn Abbey and the dissolution of the monasteries. By Gladys Scott Thomson.

161–95. The office of the English resident ambassador: its evolution as illustrated by the career of Sir Thomas Spinelly, 1509–22. By Betty Behrens. [Pp. 193–5, Appendix: List of English ambassadors employed at the Burgundian, Spanish and Imperial courts contemporaneously with Spinelly, 1509–22.]

197–210. The economic and social effects of the usury laws in the eighteenth century. By Sybil Campbell.

211–47. The English factory at Lisbon. Some chapters in its

history. By Sir Richard Lodge. [Pp. 243–5, Appendix I, 'Note on the Methuen treaties of 1703'; 246–7, Appendix II, 'Note on Abraham Castres'.]

249–62. Index.

263–308. Report of the Council, session 1931–2, etc.

Volume XVII (1934)   T 58

Pp. 1–18. PRESIDENTIAL ADDRESS. Some problems in the history of the medieval university. By F. M. Powicke.

19–48. The career of Waleran, Count of Meulan and Earl of Worcester, 1104–66. By Geoffrey H. White.

49–67. Materials for the history of the Bentivoglio signoria in Bologna. By Cecilia M. Ady.

69–100. The Anglo-Portuguese alliance. By Edgar Prestage. [Pp. 99–100, Bibliographical note.]

101–16. On the need for a new edition of Walter of Henley. By Eileen Power. [Pp. 113–16, Discussion.]

117–47. Sir John Fortescue and his theory of dominion. (*Alexander Prize Essay.*) By S. B. Chrimes.

149–76. The law merchant in England in the seventeenth and eighteenth centuries. By Miss L. Stuart Sutherland.

177–226. 'The Canningite party.' By A. Aspinall. [P. 220, Tables showing family connections; pp. 221–6, Appendix, Canningites in the Parliament of 1796–1802.]

227–42. Index.

243–308. Report of the Council, session 1932–3, etc.

Volume XVIII (1935)   T 59

Pp. 1–23. PRESIDENTIAL ADDRESS. Guy de Montfort, 1265–71. By F. M. Powicke. [Pp. 21–3, Additional note, with sketch of Neapolitan fiefs of Simon and Guy de Montfort.]

25–52. Russia and panslavism in the eighteen-seventies. By B. H. Sumner.

53–84. Faversham and the Cinque Ports. By Miss K. M. E. Murray.

85–106. The Jacobite activities in south and west England in the summer of 1715. By Sir Charles Petrie.

107–22. The Inquisitorial archives as a source of English history. By Cecil Roth.

123–42. Pierre d'Ailly and the Council of Constance, a study in 'Ockhamite' theory and practice. By Agnes E. Roberts. [Pp. 140–2, 'Appendix of illustrative passages'.]

135–68. Richard de Bury, 1287–1345. By N. Denholm-Young. [Pp. 164–8, Appendix I, Note on letters in British Museum Royal MS.12 D. XI; II, 'Bury's clerks'; III, 'Bury's preferments'.]

169–93. The chronology of labour services. By M. Postan.

195–206. Index.

207–84. Report of the Council, Session 1935–6 etc. [P. 216, Appendix, Record Society publications added to the Library.]

Volume XXI (1939)   T 62

Pp. 1–19. PRESIDENTIAL ADDRESS. The historical bearing of place-name studies; England in the sixth century. By F. M. Stenton.

21–39. The development of English medieval scholarship between 1660 and 1730. By D. C. Douglas.

41–69. The idea of a mercantile state. By A. V. Judges.

71–102. English and Čech influences on the Husite movement. By R. R. Betts.

103–31. The last years of the Court of Star Chamber, 1630–41. (*Alexander Prize Essay*.) By Henry E. I. Phillips.

133–68. Fox's martyrs: The general election of 1784. By Mrs. Eric George.

169–79. Index.

181–255. Report of the Council session, 1936–7, etc. [P. 188, Appendix, Record Society publications added to the Library.]

Volume XXII (1940)   T 63

Pp. 1–22. PRESIDENTIAL ADDRESS. The historical bearing of place-name studies: the English occupation of Southern Britain. By F. M. Stenton.

23–38. The Camden Society, 1838–1938. By Charles Johnson.

39–66. The Lincoln diocesan records. By Miss Kathleen Major.

67–99. The first house of Bellême. By Geoffrey H. White. [Appendix A, pp. 89–90, 'Richard I of Normandy and Bernard, count of Senlis; Appendix B, pp. 91–5, 'Yves de Creil and the founder of l'Abbayette'; Appendix C, pp. 96–9, 'Date of the death of Mabel de Bellême, countess of Shrewsbury'.]

101–39. Some factors in the beginnings of Parliament. By J. E. A. Jolliffe.

141–69. The deprived married clergy in Essex, 1553–61. (*Alexander Prize Essay*.) By Miss Hilda E. P. Grieve.

Volume XXV (1943)   T 66

Pp. 1–13. PRESIDENTIAL ADDRESS. The historical bearing of place-name studies: the place of women in Anglo-Saxon history. By F. M. Stenton.

15–33. Manuscripts and the war. By C. T. Flower.

35–72. The significance of the baronial reform movement, 1258–67. By R. F. Treharne.

73–91. Medieval democracy in the Brandenburg towns and its defeat in the fifteenth century. (*Alexander Prize Essay*.) By F. L. Carsten. [Sketch-map opp. p. 92.]

93–119. The study and use of Archdeacons' Court records, illustrated from the Oxford records, 1566–1759. By E. R. Brinkworth.

121–38. The new course in British foreign policy, 1892–1902. By Lillian M. Penson.

139–44. Index. 145–65. Report of Council, 1940–1, etc.

Volume XXVI (1944)   T 67

Pp. 1–12. PRESIDENTIAL ADDRESS. English families and the Norman Conquest. By F. M. Stenton.

13–35. From witness of the shire to full parliament. By Miss H. M. Cam.

37–52. Some developments in English monastic life, 1216–1336. By Dom David Knowles.

53–79. Parliament and 'bastard feudalism'. By K. B. McFarlane. [Appendix, pp. 74–9, Analysis of the returns of the Commissioners, 1412.]

80–3. Index. 84–103. Report of Council, 1941–2, etc.

Volume XXVII (1945)   T 68

Pp. 1–12. PRESIDENTIAL ADDRESS. The Scandinavian colonies in England and Normandy. By F. M. Stenton.

13–28. Pope Alexander III and the canonization of saints. (*Alexander Prize Essay*.) By E. W. Kemp.

29–39. The organization of indentured retinues in fourteenth-century England. By N. B. Lewis.

41–59. Petitions for benefices from English universities during the Great Schism. By E. F. Jacob.

61–83. Bismarck and the Three Emperors' Alliance, 1881–7. By W. N. Medlicott.

84–6. Index.

87–106. Report of the Council, session 1942–3, etc.

151–8. Index.

159–229. Report of Council, session 1947–8, etc.

Volume XXXII (1950)   T 73

Pp. 1–14. Some aspects of dynastic policy in the Balkans. By R. W. Seton-Watson. [Intended as Presidential Address in 1948 but not delivered owing to illness.]

15–30. Marriage settlements in the eighteenth century. By H. J. Habakkuk.

31–48. Anglo-Scottish relations, 1603–40. By C. Veronica Wedgwood.

49–69. The study of African history. By J. W. Blake.

71–85. The Byzantine Empire in the eleventh century: some different interpretations. By Joan M. Hussey.

87–110. The Colonial Office and the annexation of Fiji. (*Alexander Prize Essay*, 1949.) By Ethel Drus.

111–19. The Vyvyan family of Trelowarren. By Mary Coate.

121–39. Pope Boniface VIII and the commune of Orvieto. By D. P. Waley. [Opposite p. 121 is a folding map showing 'Orvieto and its sphere of influence' in the fourteenth century.]

141–51. PRESIDENTIAL ADDRESS. Deeds and seals. By T. F. T. Plucknett. [Suggestion for a *Manuel de diplomatique anglaise*.]

153–226. Report of Council, session 1948–9, etc.

FIFTH SERIES

Volume I (1951)   T 74

Pp. 1–23. Some Spanish reactions to Elizabethan colonial enterprises. By D. B. Quinn.

25–45. The work of Gregory of Tours in the light of modern research. By J. M. Wallace-Hadrill.

47–69. Peel and the party system, 1830–50. By Norman Gash.

71–89. English regular canons and the continent in the twelfth century. By J. C. Dickinson.

91–108. The results of the Rye House Plot and their influence upon the Revolution of 1688. (*Alexander Prize Essay*.) By Doreen J. Milne.

109–26. The electorate and the repeal of the Corn Laws. By G. S. R. Kitson Clark.

127–51. George III and the politicians. By R. Pares.

153–64. PRESIDENTIAL ADDRESS. The impeachments of 1376. By T. F. T. Plucknett.

165–236. Report of Council, session 1949–50, etc.

Volume II (1952)   T 75

Pp. 1–19. The Church in England between the death of Bede and the Danish invasions. By D. J. V. Fisher.

21–45. Florence and the despots. Some aspects of Florentine diplomacy in the fourteenth century. By N. Rubinstein.

47–67. The generals and the downfall of the German monarchy, 1917–18. By E. Eyck.

69–88. Edward III and the beginnings of the Hundred Years' War. By G. Templeman.

89–107. The origins of the commission system in the West India trade. (*Alexander Prize Essay*.) By K. G. Davies.

109–29. The state and landed interests in thirteenth-century France and England. By Edward Miller.

131–57. The smugglers' trade: a neglected aspect of English commercial development. By G. D. Ramsay.

159–71. PRESIDENTIAL ADDRESS. State trials under Richard II. By T. F. T. Plucknett.

173–239. Report of Council, session 1950–1, etc.

Volume III (1953)   T 76

Pp. 1–21. The Scots army in the reign of Anne. By S. H. F. Johnston.

23–39. Combination in the mid-nineteenth century coal industry. By A. J. Taylor.

41–52. Autobiographies of the middle ages. By Paul Lehmann.

53–76. Michael Davitt and the British Labour movement, 1882–1906. By T. W. Moody.

77–100. Scottish rulers and the religious orders, 1070–1153. (*Alexander Prize Essay*.) By G. W. S. Barrow. [Appendix, pp. 99–100, charters of Earl David and Earl Henry, c. 1114 and c. 1140–5.]

101–24. Sherborne, Glastonbury, and the expansion of Wessex. By H. P. R. Finberg. [Pp. 123–4, Appendix: 'The benefactors of Sherborne'.]

125–43. Political nonconformity in the eighteen-thirties. By F. R. Salter.

145–58. PRESIDENTIAL ADDRESS. Impeachment and attainder. By T. F. T. Plucknett. [In fourteenth and fifteenth centuries.]

161–228. Report of Council, session 1951–2, etc.

Volume IV (1954)   T 77

Pp. 1–17. Frankish colonization: a new approach. By Charles Verlinden.

19–43. War and finance in the Anglo-Norman state. By J. O. Prestwich.

45–68. The formation of the coalition cabinet of 1852. By C. H. Stuart.

69–89. Bristol—metropolis of the west in the eighteenth century. (*Alexander Prize Essay*.) By W. E. Minchinton.

91–109. The division of the spoils of war in fourteenth-century England. By Denys Hay.

111–34. Louis XIV and the origins of the War of the Spanish Succession. By M. A. Thomson.

135–55. PRESIDENTIAL ADDRESS. Thomas Jefferson in American historiography. By H. Hale Bellot.

157–224. Report of Council, session 1952–3, etc.

Volume V (1955)   T 78

Pp. 1–22. The King's prisons before 1250. By R. B. Pugh.

23–39. East Anglia and the Danelaw. By R. H. C. Davis.

41–59. The role of the London Missionary Society in the opening up of east central Africa. By A. J. Hanna.

61–80. North Africa and Europe in the early middle ages. By W. H. C. Frend. [With map of 'North Africa in seventh century A.D.', opp. p. 61.]

81–110. The *Oculus sacerdotis* and some other works of William of Pagula. (*Alexander Prize Essay*.) By L. E. Boyle. [Appendix A, pp. 105–8, 'Dating and sequence of the five works of William of Pagula'; Appendix B, 109–10, 'Manuscripts of the *Oculus sacerdotis* (complete or incomplete) and *Summa summarum*'.]

111–31. The re-establishment of the Church of England, 1660–3. By Anne Whiteman.

133–59. Emigration and the state, 1833–55: an essay in administrative history. By Oliver MacDonagh. [Work of Colonial Land and Emigration Commission.]

161–76. PRESIDENTIAL ADDRESS. Council and Cabinet in the mainland colonies. By H. Hale Bellot.

177–246. Report of Council, session 1953–4, etc.

Volume VI (1956)   T 79

Pp. 1–19. English provincial towns in the early sixteenth century. By W. G. Hoskins.

21–47. Empire and papacy: the last struggle. By H. S. Offler. [Lewis of Bavaria, John XXII, Benedict XII and Clement VI.]

49–68. The negotiations between Charles II and the Cardinal de Retz, 1658–9. By F. J. Routledge. [Appendix, pp. 62–8, text of letters from Charles II to the Cardinal and from de Retz to the Marquis of Ormonde, 1659.]

69–92. The political creed of Thomas Cromwell. By G. R. Elton.

93–114. The Gordon Riots: a study of the rioters and their victims. (*Alexander Prize Essay*.) By George F. E. Rudé.

115–38. The English hierarchy in the reign of Edward III. By J. R. L. Highfield.

139–60. The expansion of Liverpool's carrying trade with the Far East and Australia, 1860–1914. By Francis E. Hyde.

161–87. PRESIDENTIAL ADDRESS. The Leighs in South Carolina. By H. Hale Bellot. [Peter Leigh (1711–59), chief justice, and Egerton Leigh (1733–81), attorney-general.]

189–260. Report of Council, session 1954–5, etc.

Volume VII (1957)   T 80

Pp. 1–18. The foundation of Norwich Cathedral. By Miss B. Dodwell.

19–46. The political objectives of Gustavus Adolphus in Germany, 1630–2. By M. Roberts.

47–70. The first earl of Shaftesbury's colonial policy. By E. E. Rich.

71–89. Ivan the Terrible in Russian historiography. By G. H. Bolsover.

91–116. The investment of Sir John Fastolf's profits of war. By K. B. McFarlane.

117–36. The Folvilles of Ashby-Folville, Leicestershire, and their associates in crime, 1326–47. By E. L. G. Stones.

137–57. The organization of the Cabinet in the reign of Queen Anne. By J. H. Plumb.

159–82. PRESIDENTIAL ADDRESS. The literature of the last half-century on the constitutional history of the United States. By H. Hale Bellot.

183–216. Report of Council, session 1955–6, etc.

Volume VIII (1958) T 81

Pp. 1–20. The constitutional position of the great lordships of south Wales. By A. J. Otway-Ruthven.

21–40. Dr. Joseph Priestley, John Wilkinson and the French Revolution, 1789–1802. By W. H. Chaloner.

41–57. The early history of the Communist Party of Great Britain, 1920–9. By Henry Pelling.

59–83. The origins of the manor in England. By T. H. Aston.

85–104. The origins of the office of coroner. (*Alexander Prize Essay.*) By R. F. Hunnisett.

105–27. The Protestant constitution and its supporters, 1800–1829. By G. F. A. Best.

129–46. The new agriculture in lower Normandy, 1750–89. By Alun Davies.

147–66. PRESIDENTIAL ADDRESS. Great historical enterprises. I. The Bollandists. By M. D. Knowles.

167–82. Report of Council, session 1956–7, i–xviii, etc.

Volume IX (1959) T 82

Pp. 1–17. The English farmers of the customs, 1343–51. By E. B. Fryde.

19–49. Rank and emolument in the British diplomatic service, 1689–1789. By D. B. Horn.

51–79. The social origins and provenance of the English bishops during the reign of Edward II. By Miss K. Edwards. [Appendix, 'Letter from Katherine Paynel to John de Langton' (pp. 78–9).]

81–101. The other face of mercantilism. By Charles Wilson.

103–22. County politics and a Puritan *cause célèbre*: Somerset church ales, 1633. (*Alexander Prize Essay*.) By Thomas G. Barnes.

123–40. Commerce in the Dark Ages: a critique of the evidence. By Philip Grierson.

141–67. People and government in southern Asia. By Hugh Tinker. [From absolute monarchy to community development.]

169–87. PRESIDENTIAL ADDRESS. Great historical enterprises. II. The Maurists. By M. D. Knowles.

189–203, i–xviii. Report of Council, session 1957–8, etc.

Volume X (1960)   T 83

Pp. 1–18. Decadence or shift? Changes in the civilization of Italy and Europe in the sixteenth and seventeenth centuries. By H. G. Koenigsberger.

19–39. The treaty of Brétigny, 1360. By John Le Patourel.

41–59. The Council of the West. By Joyce A. Youings.

61–83. England and the Empire in the early twelfth century. By K. Leyser.

85–109. The origins and early history of the keeper of the peace. (*Alexander Prize Essay*.) By Alan Harding.

111–27. Edward I and the proposed purchase of English law for the Irish, *c.* 1276–80. By Aubrey Gwynn.

129–50. PRESIDENTIAL ADDRESS. Great historical enterprises. III. The *Monumenta Germaniae Historica*. By M. D. Knowles.

151–203, i–xviii. Report of Council, session 1958–9, etc.

Volume XI (1961)   T 84

Pp. 1–21. Diplomacy and war plans in the United States, 1890–1917. By J. A. S. Grenville. [P. 15, Map based on U.S. strategic map, War Plan Orange.]

23–42. Philip II and the papacy. By J. Lynch.

43–67. Les Cahorsins, hommes d'affaires français du XIIIe siècle. By Yves Renouard.

69–80. The development of the European states system since the eighteenth century. By F. H. Hinsley.

81–99. London and Edward I. (*Alexander Prize Essay*.) By Gwyn A. Williams. [Appendix, p. 99, 'The aldermanic class, *c.* 1200–1340'.]

101–15. Lloyd George and Churchill as war ministers. By John Ehrman.

117–36. John of Ford and the English Cistercian writing, 1167–1214. By C. J. Holdsworth.

137–59. PRESIDENTIAL ADDRESS. Great historical enterprise. IV. The Rolls series. By M. D. Knowles.

161–215, i–xviii. Report of Council, session 1959–60, etc.

Volume XII (1962)   T 85

Pp. 1–23. Archbishop John Stafford. By E. F. Jacob.

25–48. Profit-and-loss accountancy at Norwich Cathedral priory. By E. Stone. [P. 48, Appendix, quoting an account of Henry of Lakenham's time, fl. 1289.]

81–94. The Anglo-French peace negotiations, 1390–6. (*Alexander Prize Essay*.) By J. J. N. Palmer.

95–114. Bentham and the French Revolution. By J. H. Burns.

115–130. David II and the Government of fourteenth-century Scotland. By Bruce Webster.

131–56. PRESIDENTIAL ADDRESS. Anglo-American rivalries and Spanish American emancipation. By R. A. Humphreys.

157–215, i–xviii. Report of Council, session 1964–5, etc.

Volume XVII (1967) T 90

Pp. 1–22. Problems of the interpretation and revision of eighteenth-century Irish economic history. By L. M. Cullen.

23–40. St. Dominic and his first biographer. [Jordan of Saxony.] By C. N. L. Brooke.

41–58. The mental world of Hernán Cortés. By J. H. Elliott.

59–82. The franchise of return of writs. (*Alexander Prize Essay*.) By M. T. Clanchy. [Appendix A, p. 80, References to *non omittas*, 1200–20; Appendix B, 81, References to return of writs before 1250; Appendix C, 82, Select writ endorsements.]

83–108. Was there a Tudor despotism after all? By Joel Hurstfield.

109–30. The Norman Conquest. By R. Allen Brown.

131–64. PRESIDENTIAL ADDRESS. Anglo-American rivalries and the Venezuela crisis of 1895. By R. A. Humphreys. [P. 132, three sketch maps showing boundaries between British Guiana and Venezuela.]

165–225, i–xviii. Report of Council, session 1965–6, etc.

Volume XVIII (1968) T 91

Pp. 1–24. The losing of the initiative by the House of Commons, 1780–1914. By Valerie Cromwell.

25–48. The papacy, the patarines and the church of Milan. By H. E. J. Cowdrey.

49–68. The Mongols, the Turks and the Muslim polity. By Bernard Lewis.

69–96. The 'royal independents' in The English Civil War. By Valerie Pearl.

97–121. The *Imitation of Christ* in late medieval England, (*Alexander Prize Essay*.) By Roger W. Lovatt,

123–43. The social causes of the British industrial revolution. By H. J. Perkin.

145–73. The common lawyer in pre-Reformation England. By E. W. Ives.

174–208. PRESIDENTIAL ADDRESS. Anglo-American rivalries in Central America. By R. A. Humphreys.

209–70, i–xix. Report of Council, session 1966–7, etc.

MISCELLANEOUS PUBLICATIONS

Genealogical memoirs of the family of Sir Walter Scott, Bart. M 1 of Abbotsford, with a reprint of his *Memorials of the Haliburtons*. Houlston and Sons, Paternoster Square, London, 1877. lxxii, 78 pp., frontis. [Originally issued as a publication of the Grampian Club, reissued for the Royal Historical Society with a different title-page.]

> Pp. v–viii, Preface; ix, Contents; xi–lxii, 'Genealogical memoirs' etc.; 1–70, *Memorials* etc., with facsimile of original title-page of 1824; 71–8, Index to whole vol.

Genealogical memoirs of the Scottish house of Christie. M 2 Compiled from family papers and the public records by Charles Rogers. Printed for the Royal Historical Society, 1878. 78 pp.

> Pp. 3–4, Preface; 5–71, 'Genealogical memoirs'; 73–8, Index.

Genealogical memoirs of John Knox and of the family of M 3 Knox. By Charles Rogers. Printed for the Royal Historical Society, 1879. 184 pp. [Also issued by the Grampian Club.]

> Pp. iii–iv, Preface; 5–166, 'Genealogical memoirs'; 167–72, Appendix (on various Knoxes); 173–84, Index.

Genealogical memoirs of the families of Colt and Coutts. By M 4 Charles Rogers. Printed for the Royal Historical Society, 1879. 59 pp. [Also issued by the Cottonian Society, 1879.]

Domesday Commemoration, 1886. Notes on the manuscripts M 5 etc. exhibited at H.M. Public Record Office. Issued under the direction of the Domesday Commemoration Committee of the Royal Historical Society, 1886. Reprinted in *Domesday studies*, Vol. II (1891), pp. 621–47. *See* M 9(*b*) *below*. Three folio sheets listing *Printed books exhibited in the British Museum* for the Commemoration were also printed (1886) and later incorporated in *Domesday studies*, Vol. II (1891), pp. 649–62. *See* M 9(*b*) *below*.

the Royal Historical Society, with notes and tables by I. S. Leadam. Longmans, Green, 1897. 2 vols.

Vol. I. Pp. 1–80, General introduction; 81–388, Latin texts of inquisitions for Berks, Bucks, Essex, Leics., Lincs., Northants, Oxon., with notes. *(a)*

Vol. II. Pp. 389–476, Latin texts of inquisitions for Warwicks. and Beds., with notes; 477–98, Appendices I–IX, parallel and illustrative MSS.; 499–639, statistical tables, Berks. and Bucks; 640–44, inquisition of 1517 for Cheshire; 645–93, The inquisitions of 1517, 1518 and 1549 for Warwickshire from the Dugdale MSS.; 695–715, Index. *(b)*

A bibliography of the historical works of Dr. Creighton, late bishop of London, Dr. Stubbs, late bishop of Oxford, Dr. S. R. Gardiner and the late Lord Acton. *Ed.* W. A. Shaw. Royal Historical Society, 1903. 63 pp. M 12

P. iii, Contents; v, Preface by G. W. Prothero; pp. 9–14, list of Creighton's works; 17–23, list of Stubbs's; 27–39, list of Gardiner's; 43–63, list of Acton's.

Catalogue of the library of the Royal Historical Society. Printed for the Fellows of the Royal Historical Society, 22 Russell Square, London, W.C., 1915. v, 83 pp. M 13

Pp. iii–iv, Preface; v, 'Rules for borrowers'; 1–63, Printed books; 64–73, Publications of societies and academies; 74–5, Periodicals; 76, Atlases and maps; 77–83, Manuscripts.

German opinion and German policy before the War. By Sir G. W. Prothero. R.H.S. 1916, iv, 86 pp. M 14

Expanded from a lecture given before the Society on 21 January, 1915.

Magna Carta commemoration essays. With a preface by Viscount Bryce. *Ed.* Henry Elliot Malden. R.H.S. 1917. xxxi, 311 pp. M 15

Pp. vii–ix, Magna Carta celebration, 1915: General Committee nominated in 1914; ix–xviii, Preface by Lord Bryce; xix–xxxi, Introduction by H. E. Malden; 1–25, 'Magna Carta, 1215–1915', an address delivered on its seventh centenary to the Royal Historical Society and the Magna Carta Celebration Committee', by William S. McKechnie; 26–45, 'Innocent III and the Great Charter', by G. B. Adams (pp. 41–5, Appendix quoting the Pope's letter to the Barons, 18 June 1215); 46–77, ' "Barons" and "knights" in the Great Charter', by J. H. Round; 78–95, Magna Carta c29 *Nullus liber homo* etc., by Sir P. Vinogradoff; 96–121, *Per iudicium parium vel per legem terrae*, by F. M. Powicke; 122–79, 'Magna Carta and common law', by C. H. McIlwain; 180–226, 'The influence of Magna Carta on American constitutional development', by H. D. Hazeltine; 227–43, 'Magna Carta and Spanish medieval jurisprudence', by Rafael Altamira; 244–300, 'Financial records of the reign of King John', by C. Hilary Jenkinson; 301–10, Index.

A repertory of British archives. Part I, England. Compiled **M 16** for the Royal Historical Society by Hubert Hall, assisted by research students of the University of London. R.H.S., 1920. lvi, 266 pp. [No further parts were issued.]

Pp. v–viii, Preface; ix–xxxiii, Introduction; xxxiv–xliii, Appendix to the Introduction, 'The Royal Commission of 1910 and subsequent proceedings on behalf of the preservation of public and local records in England and Wales', by Henry R. Tedder; xlv–lvi, key to principal abbreviations; 1–89, Part I, a select classified list of public records; 91–158, Part II, a survey of local records; 159–254, a directory of English archives; 255–6, Appendix A, summary list of English archives; 257–60, Appendix B, list of municipal and reputed boroughs; 261–2, Appendix C, bibliographical note; 263–6, Index.

Official information respecting the Society. Aberdeen, printed **M 17** for the R.H.S., 1921. 62 pp.

List and index of the publications of the Royal Historical **M 18** Society, 1871–1924, and of the Camden Society, 1840–97. *Ed.* Hubert Hall. R.H.S., 1925. xvii, 110 pp.

The Domesday Monachorum of Christ Church, Canterbury. **M 19** Edited with an introduction by David C. Douglas. R.H.S., 1944. 4to. v, 127 pp. + 16 plates.

P. iii, Preface; v, Contents; 1–73, Introduction; 76, 'Note on the text'; 77–110, transcript of Latin text with footnotes and extracts of entries in Domesday Book and St. Augustine's Survey concerning places mentioned; 111–27, Index. Plates are facsimiles of the complete text.

BIBLIOGRAPHY OF BRITISH HISTORY

Issued in conjunction with the American Historical Association.

Bibliography of British History. Tudor period, 1485–1603. **B 1(i)** Issued under the direction of the American Historical Association and the Royal Historical Society of Great Britain. *Ed.* Conyers Read. Oxford, Clarendon Press, 1933.

Bibliography of British History. Tudor period, 1485–1603. . . . **B 1(ii)** *Ed.* Conyers Read. Second Edition. Oxford, Clarendon Press, 1959. xxviii, 624 pp.

Pp. vii–x, Introduction; xi–xii, Preface to 2nd edn.; xiii–xvi, Preface to 1st edn.; xvii–xxvi, Contents; xxvii–xxviii, Abbreviations; 1–544, Annotated list of titles; 545–624, Index.

Bibliography of British History. Stuart period, 1603–1714. B 2
Issued under the direction of the Royal Historical Society and
the American Historical Association. *Ed.* Godfrey Davies.
Oxford, Clarendon Press, 1928. x, 460 pp.

Pp. v–vi, Contents; vii–x, Introduction; 1–385, Annotated lists of titles;
387–459, Index.

Bibliography of British History. The eighteenth century, B 3
1714–89. Issued under the direction of the American Historical
Association and the Royal Historical Society of Great Britain.
Ed. Stanley Pargellis and D. J. Medley. Oxford, Clarendon
Press, 1951. xxvi, 643 pp.

Pp. v–viii, Preface; ix–xxiv, Contents; xxv–xxvi, Abbreviations; 1–529,
Annotated lists of titles; 531–642, Index.

ANNUAL BIBLIOGRAPHIES

Writings on British history, 1934. A bibliography of books W 1
and articles on the history of Great Britain from about 450 A.D.
to 1914, published during the year 1934, with an Appendix containing a select list of publications in 1934 on British history
since 1914. Compiled by Alexander Taylor Milne. Cape, 1937.
427 pp.

Writings on British history, 1935. A bibliography . . . [for] W 2
1935 with an Appendix containing a select list of publications in
1935, on British history since 1914. Compiled by A. T. Milne.
Cape, 1939. 427 pp.

Writings on British history, 1936. A bibliography . . . . [for] W 3
1936 with an Appendix containing a select list of publications in
1936, on British history since 1914. Compiled by A. T. Milne.
Cape, 1940. 389 pp.

Writings on British history, 1937. A bibliography . . . [for] W 4
1937 with an Appendix containing a select list of publications in
1937, on British history since 1914. Compiled by A. T. Milne.
Cape, 1949. 346 pp.

Writings on British history, 1938. A bibliography . . . [for] W 5
1938 with an Appendix containing a select list of publications in
1938, on British history since 1914. Compiled by A. T. Milne.
Cape, 1951. 333 pp.

Writings on British history, 1939. A bibliography . . . [for] W 6

1939 with an Appendix containing a select list of publications in 1939, on British history since 1914. Compiled by A. T. Milne. Cape, 1953. 310 pp.

Writings on British history, 1940–5. A bibliography of books W 7 and articles on the history of Great Britain from about A.D. 450 to 1914, published during the years 1940–5, with an Appendix containing a select list of publications in these years on British history since 1914. Compiled by A. T. Milne. Cape, 1960. 2 vols.

Writings on British History, 1901–33. [Ed. H. Hale Bellot]. W 8 Cape, 1968. [*In press.* 5 in 7 volumes.]

GUIDES AND HANDBOOKS

No. 1 G 1

Guide to English commerical statistics, 1696–1782. By G. N. Clark. With a catalogue of materials by Barbara M. Franks. R.H.S., 1938. xvi, 211 pp.

Pp. ix–xvi, Introduction, including (xi–xvi) 'Statistics based on the yield of the Customs'; 1–42, 'The Inspectors-General of Imports and Exports'; 43–4, 'The bills of entry'; 45–51, 'The general registers of shipping'; 52–6, 'Note on the Port Books'; 57–150, 'Appendix of documents' (extracts and tables); 151–206, 'Catalogue of statistical material' (with short Introduction); 207–211, Index.

No. 2 G 2 (i)

Handbook of British chronology. *Ed.* F. M. Powicke, with the assistance of Charles Johnson and W. J. Harte. R.H.S., 1939. xii, 424 pp.

Pp. v–vi, Table of contents; vii–x, Preface; xi–xii, List of principal abbreviations; 1–63, lists of 'Independent rulers', with introductions, and notes; 64–106, 'English officers of state'; 107–28, Ireland—Chief Governors (1172–1939) and Deputies (1211–1800), Secretaries of State and Keepers of the Signet or Privy Seal (1560–1829); 129–31, the Channel Islands; 132–288, the succession of bishops—archbishops and bishops of the provinces of Canterbury and York, Wales (lists of bishops), Scotland (lists of Scottish bishops), Ireland (lists of archbishops and bishops, including Catholic archbishops and bishops of Ireland from the Reformation); 289–338, Alphabetical list of dukes, marquesses and earls (1066–1603); 339–50, English parliaments (1258–1547); 351–71, Provincial and national councils of the Church (602–1536); 373–97, Reckonings of time and the beginning of the year; 398–419, Saints' days and festivals used in dating; 420–4, Legal chronology.

No. 2 G 2 (ii)

Handbook of British chronology. *Ed.* Sir F. Maurice Powicke
and E. B. Fryde. Second edition. R.H.S., 1961. xxxviii, 565 pp.

Pp. v–viii, Table of contents; ix–xi, preface to 1st edn.; xiii–xvi, preface
to 2nd edn.; xvii–xix, list of abbreviations; xxi–xxxviii, 'Bibliographical
guide to the lists of English office-holders (to *c.* 1800)'; 1–64, 'Independent rulers'; 65–146, 'English officers of state'; 147–68, 'Ireland—Chief
Governors and deputies (1172–1952)'; 169–71, 'Chief Secretaries in Ireland (1566–1922)'; 172–98, 'Scottish officers of state (*c.* 1123–1955)';
199–201, 'A note on the Channel Islands'; 202–72, 'Archbishops and
bishops of England' (597–1956); 273–80, 'Bishops of Wales' (1090–
1956); 281–301, 'Bishops of Scotland to 1689'; 302–79, 'Archbishops
and bishops of Ireland to 1534'; 379–412, 'Roman Catholic archbishops
and bishops from 1534'; 413–56, 'Dukes, marquesses and earls (Scotland)'; 492–544, 'English and British parliaments and related assemblies
to 1832'; 545–65, 'Provincial and national councils of the Church of
England (602–1536)'.

No. 3 G 3 (i)

Medieval libraries of Great Britain. A list of surviving books.
Ed. N. R. Ker. R.H.S., 1951. xxiv, 169 pp.

Pp. vii–xxxiii, Preface; xxiv, Principal abbreviations; 1–120, list of
surviving books; 121–3, Appendix: books formerly owned by parish
churches and chapels; 125–66, Index of manuscripts; 167–8, Index of
printed books; 169, Index of untraced manuscripts and printed books.

No. 3 G 3 (ii)

Medieval libraries of Great Britain. A list of surviving books.
Ed. N. R. Ker. Second edition. R.H.S., 1964. xxxii, 424 pp.

Pp. vii–xxiii, Revised preface to the first edition; xxv–xxix, Preface to
the second edition; xxx–xxxi, Principal abbreviations and conventional
signs; xxxii, *addenda*; 1–218, list of surviving books; 219–24, Appendix:
books formerly owned by parish churches and chapels; 225–321, 'Donors,
scribes and other persons concerned before 1540 with the books recorded on pp. 1–224'; 322–5, 'Donors and other persons concerned with
books formerly owned by parish churches and chapels'; 326–31, 'Glossary
of words used in references to books and ownership recorded on pp. 225–
325'; 332–95, Index of manuscripts; 396–402, Index of printed books;
403–4, Index of untraced manuscripts and printed books; 405–24, Index
of personal names.

No. 4 G 4

Handbook of dates for students of English history. *Ed.* C. R.
Cheney. R.H.S., 1945. xvii, 164 pp. Reprinted 1948, 1955.

Pp. vii–x, Preface; xi–xvii, Select bibliography; 1–11, Reckonings of time; 12–31, Rulers of England and regnal years; 32, Exchequer years of English rulers; 33–9, list of popes from Gregory the Great to Pius XII (590–1939); 40–64, Saints' days and festivals used in dating; 65–74, Legal chronology; 75–81, The Roman calendar; 83–161, Calendar for all possible dates of Easter; 163–4, Index.

No. 5   G 5

Guide to the national and provincial directories of England and Wales, excluding London, published before 1856. By Jane E. Norton. R.H.S., 1950. vii, 241 pp.

Pp. v–vi, Preface; 1–24, Introduction; 27–225, Catalogue of directories, with notes; 226, Addenda; 227–37, Index of authors, publishers and printers; 239–41, General Index.

No. 6   G 6

Handbook of oriental history. By members of the Department of Oriental History, School of Oriental and African Studies, University of London. *Ed.* C. H. Philips. R.H.S., 1951. viii, 265 pp.

Pp. vii–viii, Preface; 1–46, Section I, The Near and Middle East, by Bernard Lewis; 47–95, Section II, India and Pakistan, by C. H. Philips; 97–152, Section III, South-east Asia and the Archipelago, by D. G. E. Hall; 153–214, Section IV, China, by O. P. N. B. Van der Sprenkel; 215–39, Section V, Japan, by W. G. Beasley; 241–65, Alphabetical list of dynasties and rulers.

No. 7   G 7

Texts and calendars. An analytical guide to serial publications. By E. L. C. Mullins. R.H.S., 1958. xi, 674 pp.

Pp. v–viii, Preface; ix–xi, Contents; 3–93, Part I, publications of official bodies; 97–285, Part II, national societies; 289–513, Part III, English local societies; 517–31, Part IV, Welsh societies; 535–7, Part V, *addenda*; 539–670, Index; 671–4, 'Books not in the Society's library' (i.e. among those listed in the work).

No. 8

Anglo-Saxon charters. An annotated list and bibliography. By P. H. Sawyer. R.H.S., 1968. xiii, 538 pp.

Pp. vii–xi, Preface; xiii, Principal abbreviations and conventional signs; 1–25, Bibliography and bibliographical abbreviations; 26–43, Concordances with the principal editions; 44–67, The manuscripts (containing the charters listed); 68, Printed sources; 69–441, Lists of charters, miscellaneous grants, wills, etc.; 442–83, lost and incomplete texts; 485–538, Index of persons and places.

GENERAL INDEX

Names of authors and editors are in SMALL CAPITALS. References to the volumes listed above are arranged under each heading in numerical order, items in Camden volumes being noted first, followed by any in the *Transactions* and other publications of the Society.

The various series are explained in the Preface. It should be noted here that direct reference to the volumes in them can be made from this Index if the following key to the numbering and abbreviations is used:

Camden Society and Camden series

Old series, vols. 1–105	C 1 – C 105
New series, vols. 1–62	C 106 – C 167
Third series, vols. 1–94	C 168 – C 261
Fourth series, vols. 1–4	C 262 – C 265
Catalogues of Camden old series	CX 1 – CX 3

Royal Historical Society Transactions

Old series, vols. 1–10	T 1 – T 10
New series, vols. 1–20	T 11 – T 30
Third series, vols. 1–11	T 31 – T 41
Fourth series, vols. 1–33	T 42 – T 73
Fifth series, vols. 1–18	T 74 – T 91
Miscellaneous Publications	M 1 – M 19
Bibliography of British history	B 1 – B 3
Annual Bibliographies	W 1 – W 8
Guides and Handbooks	G 1 – G 8

Aberconway, abbey of, register and chronicle of, C 39(*a*)

ABERDARE, LORD. *See* BRUCE, HENRY A.

Aberdeen, earl of. *See* Gordon, George Hamilton

Abingdon Abbey, Obedientiars' accounts of (14th–16th c.), C 156

Accountancy, in Wardrobe of Edward I, T 47 p. 50; in Wardrobe of Edward II, T 53 p. 75

Accounts, John of Brabant's (1292–3), C 55(*a*); farming (1610–20), C 220; fascimile of farm, C 220 frontis.; of Percy household (1546–1632), C 260

ACKERS, B. ST. JOHN, on education of deaf, T 8 p. 163

Acton, *Sir* John Emerich Dalberg, *1st Baron Acton* (d. 1902), bibliography of his historical works, M 12 p. 43

Arresta facta apud Tholosam (1270), T 52 p. 176

Art, renaissance of, in Italy, T 3 p. 408

Arthur, King, early English metrical romances on, C 18

Arts, fine, under Puritans, T 15 p. 205

ASHLEY, PERCY, on study of 19th c. history, T 30 p. 133

Asia, people and government in southern (18th–20th c.), T 82 p. 141; south-east, treated in *Handbook of oriental history*, G 6 p. 97

ASPINALL, ARTHUR, *ed.* corresp. on formation of Canning's ministry (1827), C 226; *ed.* corresp. of Charles Arbuthnot, C 232; on the Canningite party, T 58 p. 177

Assassination, and history, T 14 p. 285

Assertio septem sacramentorum, by King Henry VIII, T 8 p. 242

Assizes, account book of T. Walmysley while riding western and Oxford circuit (1596–1601), C 73(*b*)

Assurance, life, in Britain, T 3 p. 372

ASTON, TREVOR HENRY, on origins of the manor in England, T 81 p. 59

Atlantis, legend of, T 13 p. 1

Attainder, impeachment and (14th–15th c.), T 76 p. 145

Atterbury, Francis (d. 1732), letters from A. Pope, received in Tower of London by, C 73(*f*)

ATTHILL, WILLIAM, *ed.* documents relating to Middleham church, C 38

Aubrey, John (d. 1697), extracts from 'Remains of Gentilism and Judaism', unpublished work partly by him, etc., C 5 p. 80

Auditing, medieval, *regimen scaccarii* in English monasteries, T 65 p. 73

Augustinian order, dissolution of house at Christchurch, Aldgate, T 49 p. 127

AUNGIER, GEORGE JAMES, *ed.* anonymous *Croniques de Londres*, C 28

Australia, war records of (1914–18), T 44 p. 41; Liverpool's carrying trade with (1860–1914), T 79 p. 139

Austria, royal house of, T 12 p. 225; British relations with, T 41 p. 1; Family, Court and State Archives of, in Vienna, T 45 p. 49

Austrian Succession, War of the, T 50 p. 63

Autobiographies, medieval, T 76 p. 41

Autographs, Tite Collection of 17th c., C 87(*d*)

Avery, Joseph, diplomatic correspondence of (1640–2), T. 25 p. 151

AYLMER, GERALD EDWARD, on place-bills and separation of powers: origins of non-political civil service (17th c.), T 88 p. 45

Aytoun, *Sir* Robert (d. 1638), memoir and poems of, T 1, p. 96

Babington, Anthony (d. 1586), letter from Mary, Queen of Scots to (1586), C 184 p. 129; conspiracy of, T 32 p. 184

Babthorpe family, pedigree of, C 4 p. ci

CAULFIELD, RICHARD, *ed.* Journal of Rowland Davies (1688–90), C 68

Cavendish, Henry (d. 1616), Fox's account of his journey to Constantinople (1589), C 231(*b*)

Cavendish, *Sir* William (d. 1557), accounts of, while Treasurer of the Chamber, C 84 p. 1

Cecil, *Sir* Edward, *Viscount Wimbledon* (d. 1638), Glanville's journal of Cadiz expedition commanded by (1625), C 137; letters to Sir J. Coke from (1625–6), C 137 p. xxxiii

Cecil, *Sir* Robert, *1st earl of Salisbury* (d. 1612), correspondence of James VI of Scotland with, C 78; Letters to Carew from (1600–1603), C 88

Cecil, Robert A. T. Gascoyne, *3rd marquess of Salisbury*, (d. 1903), foreign policy of, T 66 p. 121

Cecil, William, *Baron Burghley* (d. 1598), as Master of the Court of Wards, T 72 p. 95

Cecilia, Princess of Sweden, her visit to Elizabeth I, T 22 p. 181

Celtic church, and English Christianity, T 11 p. 376

Celts, dynastic achievement in England of, T 13 p. 343

Cely family, papers of (1475–88), C 168; letter from correspondence of, T 40 p. 159

Central America, Anglo-American rivalries in, T 91 p. 174

Ceremonies, inauguration, of Yorkist Kings, T 71 p. 51

Ceylon, expedition to (1803), T 42 p. 92

CHALONER, WILLIAM HENRY, on Priestley, Wilkinson and French Revolution (1789–1802), T 81 p. 21

Chamberlain, John (d. 1627), News letters of (1597–1603), C 79

CHAMBERS, RAYMOND WILSON, reply to criticisms of his *Widsith* text by, T 39 p. 156

CHANCE, JAMES FREDERICK, *ed.* British diplomatic instructions, Sweden (1689–1789), C 199, C 206; *ed.* diplomatic instructions, Denmark (1689–1789), C 203; on northern treaties (1719–20), T 31 p. 99; on Germany (early 18th c.), T 40 p. 25

Chantries, in later middle ages, T 69 p. 47

Chapel Royal, old cheque-book of (1561–1744), C 108

CHAPLAIS, PIERRE, *ed.* documents (1361–9) on treaty of Brétigny, C 247(*a*); *ed.* War of Saint-Sardos (1323–5), C 254

CHAPMAN, ANNIE BEATRICE WALLIS, *joint ed.*, English merchants and Spanish Inquisition, C 190; on Anglo-Portuguese commercial relations, T 31 p. 157; on Spanish Inquisition in Canaries, T 33 p. 237

CHAPMAN, JOHN HENRY, on Elizabethan persecution of recusants, T 9 p. 21

Charles 1, King of England etc. (d. 1649); letters to Henrietta Maria of, C 63; his Spanish marriage negotiations (1617–23), C 101, C 104(*b*); his Ripon treaty with Covenanters (1640), C 100; his

Dark Ages, evidence for commerce in, T 82 p. 123

DARLINGTON, REGINALD RALPH, ed. *Vita Wulfstani*, etc., C 207

DAVENPORT, FRANCES G., on decay of villeinage, T 24 p. 123

Davers, Mary Magdaline, letter of 3 Feb. 1613 so signed, C 87(*f*)

David I, King of Scotland (d. 1153), and religious orders, T 76 p. 77

David II, King of Scotland (d. 1371), and government of 14th c. Scotland, T 89 p. 115

Davidson, John, of Prestonpans (d. 1603), Scottish reformer, T 3 p. 163

DAVIES, ALUN, on new agriculture in lower Normandy (1750–89), T 81 p. 129

DAVIES, CUTHBERT COLLIN, ed. Macartney corresp. (1781–5), C 244; ed. Benares diary of Warren Hastings, C 246(*a*)

DAVIES, GODFREY, ed. autobiog. of Thomas Raymond and memoirs of Guise family (16th–17th c.), C 195; on Whigs and Peninsular War (1804–14), T 43 p. 113; ed. *Bibliography of British history, Stuart period*, B 2

DAVIES, JAMES CONWAY, on Despenser War in Glamorgan (1321), T 39 p. 21

DAVIES, JOHN SILVESTER, ed. English chronicle of reigns of Richard II – Henry VI, C 64

DAVIES, KENNETH GORDON, on commission system in West India trade, T 75 p. 89

DAVIES, ROBERT, ed. Life of Marmaduke Rawdon, C 85

Davies, Rowland, journal of (1688–90), C 68

DAVIS, ELIZA JEFFRIES, on dissolution of Christchurch, Aldgate, London (1532), T 49 p. 127

Davis, John, of Worcester (fl. 1550), biography of, C 77 p. 68

DAVIS, RALPH HENRY CARLESS, ed. Kalendar of Abbot Samson etc., C 251; on East Anglia and Danelaw, T 78 p. 23

Davitt, Michael (d. 1906), and British Labour movement, T 76 p. 53

DAWSON, WILLIAM, on Celtic church, T 11 p. 376

De nugis curialium (Walter Map's), C 50

Deaf, education of, T 8 p. 163

DEANESLY, MARGARET, on early English and Gallic minsters, T 64 p. 25

Dedham classis, minute-book of (1582–9), C 175

Dee, John (d. 1608), his private diary and catalogue of MSS., C 19

Deeds, study of forms of, T 73 p. 141

Defender of the Faith, title of, T 8 p. 242

Defensor pacis, authorship of, T 50 p. 85

Degrevant, early English metrical romance, C 30

Delamer (Delamere), Lord. *See* Booth, George

Demesne, ancient, and Domesday Book, M9 (*b*) p. 471

Denarius Sancti Petri, T 25 p. 171; T 29 p. 209

Dengemarsh, Kent, rentals etc. of (13th c.), C 146

Spanish reactions to English colonial enterprises during her reign, T 74 p. 1

Elizabeth, Czarina of Russia (d. 1762), Bestucheff's *Système politique* addressed to (*c*. 1744–5), C 169 p. 241

ELLACOMBE, HENRY THOMAS, *joint ed.* wills, etc. of Richard, bishop of London (1303), and Thomas, bishop of Exeter (1310), C 115

Elliot, Hugh (d. 1830), despatches on Danish revolution (1784), C 140 p. 235; diplomatic instructions to, in Denmark (1779–89), C 203 p. 192; as minister at Berlin, T 14 p. 85

ELLIOTT, GEORGE PERCY, *ed.* Diary of Dr. E. Lake (1677–8), C 39(*f*); *ed.* W. Taswell's Autobiography (1651–82), C 55(*f*)

ELLIOTT, JOHN HUXTABLE, on Hernan Cortés, T 90 p. 41

ELLIS, *Sir* HENRY (d. 1869), *ed.* Norden's *Essex* (1594), C 9; *ed.* Original letters of eminent literary men, C 23; *ed.* part of P. Vergil's *Anglica historia* translated, C 29; C 36; *ed.* Register and chronicle of Aberconway Abbey, C 39(*a*); *ed.* Visitation of Huntingdon by N. Charles, Lancaster herald (1613), C 43; *ed.* *Obituary of Richard Smith*, C 44; *ed.* *Pilgrymage of Sir Richard Guylforde*, C 51

Ellis, John (d. 1738), letters of Humphrey Prideaux to (1674–1722), C 120

Elliston family, pedigree of, C 109 p. 258

Elmore, Glos., Guise family of, C 195 p. 102

Elsing(e), Henry (d. 1654), notes of debates in House of Lords by (1621–2), C 103; (1624, 1626), C 129; (1621, 1625, 1628), C 209; on his notes of 1628 debates, T 49 p. 38

Elsynge. *See* Elsing

ELTON, GEOFFREY RUDOLPH, on political creed of Thomas Cromwell, T 79 p. 69

Ely Cathedral, chapter ordinances and visitation records of (1241–1515), C 231(*a*); *Liber Eliensis* of priory of, C 259

Ely, diocese of, administration during vacancies (1298–9, 1302–3), T 53 p. 49

Ely, William of (d. 1215), T 56 p. 45

Embajada Española, Spanish guide to diplomacy (late 17th c.), C 204(*b*)

Emigration, movement to remedy abuses on vessels to America used for (19th c.), T 55 p. 197; and the state (1833–55), T 78 p. 133

Emma, queen (d. 1052), edn. of *Encomium Emmae Reginae*, C 239

Empire, British, discussion of problems of, in parliament (1880–5), T 86 p. 29

Empire, Holy Roman, and Papacy (14th c.), T 79 p. 21; England and (early 12th c.), T 83 p. 61; reflections on, T 87 p. 89; ambassadors at court of (1509–22), T 57 p. 161

Fortescue, *Sir* John (d. 1476?), influence of his writings, T 40 p. 77; and his theory of dominion, T 58 p. 117

FORTESCUE, *Sir* JOHN WILLIAM (d. 1933), presidential address of: (1925) on the human element in historical research, T 49 p. 1

Fortescue papers (1607–44), C 106

FOSTER, *Sir* WILLIAM, on India Board (1784–1858), T 41 p. 61

Fotherby, Thomas, diplomatic instructions to, in Denmark (1689–1701), C 203 p. 1

FOWLER, ROBERT COPP, on secular aid for excommunication, T 38 p. 113

Fox, author of Henry Cavendish's journey to Constantinople (1589), C 231(*b*)

Fox, Charles James (d. 1806), his 'martyrs' in election of 1784, T 62 p. 133

FOX, EVELYN, on diary of Elizabethan gentlewoman, T 32 p. 153

FOX, JOHN CHARLES, *ed.* diary of A. Williamson (1722–47), C 189

FOXCROFT, HELEN CHARLOTTE, *ed.* letters of Gilbert Burnet (Burnett), C 180(*a*)

Foxe, John (d. 1587), extracts from his narratives of Reformation days, C 77; on the martyrologist, T 5 p. 28

Foxe family, T 5 p. 28

France, medieval:—documents on treaty of Brétigny (1360), C 247(*a*); negotiations with England at Bruges (1374–7), C 247(*b*); Jacquerie in, T 1 p. 187; in the middle ages, T 16 p. 109; in 13th c., T 24 p. 53; early minsters in, T 64 p. 25; state and landed interests in (13 c.), T 75 p. 109; use of historical writing for war propaganda in (15th c.), T 88 p. 1; peace negotiations between England and (1390–6), T 89 p. 81

France, modern (from 1500):—Grey's surrender of Guisnes to (1558), C 40 p. 62; Buckingham's loan of ships to, C 150 p. 139; R. Ferrier's travel journal in (1687), C 158(*g*); visits by Sir T. Hoby to (1547–64), C 171(*b*); despatches of W. Perwich from (1669–77), C 172; formation of 3rd Coalition against (1804–5), C 174; despatches from Lord Dorset and others in (1784–90), C 183, C 186; diplomatic instructions to British envoys in (1689–1789), C 202, C 205, C 210, C 216; account of Terror in (1793–4), C 208 (*f*); during 17th c., T 9 p. 216, T 15 p. 147, T 25 p. 131; commercial treaty between Britain and (1786), T 12 p. 349; and Oliver Cromwell, T 15 p. 147; projected invasion of England by (1768–70), T 34 p. 83; meeting of Estates (1590), T 39 p. 65; exploration of Canada by, T 41 p. 143; archives of, during war (1914–18), T 44 p. 27; proposed treaty with Britain and America on Cuba (1852), T 54 p. 149; siege of Rouen in (1562), T 56 p. 163; British despatches on relations with (1803), M 6

Francesco de Jesus, F., edn. and trans. of his *Del matrimonio pretendido,* C 101

Oxford, Archdeacons' Court records of (1566–1759), T 66 p. 93

Oxford University, register of visitors to (1647–58), C 134; orders, expulsions, etc., C 134 p. 441; visitation of (1660–2), C 246(c); John Wycliffe and Canterbury Hall in, T 38 p. 55; Robert Bacon and Dominican school at, T 71 p. 1; Oliver Sutton and, T 72 p. 1

Packer, John (d. 1649), state letters collected by, C 106

Padua, English students at university of (15th c.), T 60 p. 101

Page, John (*fl.* 1418), poem on siege of Rouen by, C 122 p. 1

Pakistan, treated in *Handbook of oriental history*, G 6 p. 47

Palestine (16th c.), T 3 p. 346; Daniel of Kiev's journey to (*c.* 1106–7), T 24 p. 175

PALMER, J. FOSTER, on plague, T 11 p. 242; on Saxon invasion, T 12 p. 173; on Spola (1849), T 15 p. 177; on fine arts under Puritans, T 15 p. 205

PALMER, JOHN JOSEPH NORMAN, on Anglo-French peace negotiations (1390–6), T 89 p. 81

Palmer, Josceline (Julins), martyr (d. 1556), C 77 p. 85

Palmerston, Lord. *See* Temple, Henry John

Panslavism, Russia and (1870s), T 59 p. 25

PANTIN, WILLIAM ABEL, *ed.* documents on English Black Monks (1215–1540), C 212, C 214, C 221; on Benedictines in England, T 51 p. 195

Papacy, medieval, T 25 p. 171; T 29 p. 209; petitions for benefices during Great Schism, T 68 p. 41; King John and Interdict of (1208), T 72 p. 129; and commune of Orvieto, T 73 p. 121; and Holy Roman Empire (14th c.), T 79 p. 21; Philip II and, T 84 p. 23; church of Milan, patarines and, T 91 p. 25; lists of popes (590–1939), G 4 p. 33

Paper Office, report on state of (1674), C 114 p. 159

Pará, Brazil, T 44 p. 52

PARES, RICHARD, on manning of Navy in West Indies (1702–63), T 61 p. 31; on George III and the politicians, T 74 p. 127

PARGELLIS, STANLEY, ed. *Bibliography of British history: eighteenth century*, B 3

Paris, *parlement* of, medieval registers of, T 51 p. 55

Paris, peace of (1763), T 32 p. 235

Paris, Matthew (d. 1259), Magna Carta in chronicle of, T 87 p. 67

PARKER, JAMES, on church in Domesday Book, M 9(*b*) p. 399

Parlement, at Toulouse (1270), T 52 p. 176

Parlement, of Paris, Saint-Sardos tried before, C 254 p. 253; English history in registers of, T 51 p. 55

Parliament. *See also* House of Commons *and* House of Lords

Parliament, in general:—emergence of majority rule in elections to, T 87 p. 175; emergence of majority rule in Commons' procedure, T 88 p. 165; initiation of legislation in, T 91 p. 1

Rutherford, Andrew, *1st earl of Teviot* (d. 1664), letters to Lauderdale of, C 136(*f*)

RUTHVEN, A. J. OTWAY. *See* OTWAY-RUTHVEN

Rutland papers, *ed.* W. Jerdan, C 21

RYAN, ANTHONY NICHOLAS, on trade with enemy in Scandinavian and Baltic ports during Napoleonic wars, T 85 p. 123

Ryder, Dudley, *1st earl of Harrowby* (d. 1847), despatches on his Berlin mission (1804–5), C 174 p. 205

Rye House Plot, and Revolution of 1688, T 74 p. 91

Ryswick, treaty of (1697), T 55 p. 225

SACHSE, WILLIAM L., *ed.* Diurnal of Thomas Rugg (1659–61), C 258

Sackville, John Frederick, *3rd duke of Dorset* (d. 1799), despatches from France of (1784–9), C 183; his diplomatic instructions in France (1784–9), C 216 p. 248

St. Albans Abbey, courts and court rolls of, T 48 p. 52; chroniclers in, and Magna Carta, T 87 p. 67

St. Gregory's priory, Canterbury, cartulary of, C 255

St. John, Order of Knights of, T 3 p. 395

St. John, Henry, *1st viscount Bolingbroke* (d. 1751), his diplomatic instructions in France (1712), C 202 p. 25

St. Mary Clerkenwell, London, cartulary of, C 238

St. Mary's priory, Worcester, register of, C 91

St. Martin le Grand, London, cartulary of, T 60 p. 80

St. Michael's, Cornhill, churchwardens' accounts of, C 102 p. 169

St. Michael's church, Bath, churchwardens' accounts of, T 7 p. 309

St. Paul's Cathedral, London, Domesday of (1222) and other documents on manors and churches belonging to, C 69; early charters of, C 225; sermon by boy-bishop at (*temp.* Henry VIII), C 119(*a*); documents illustrating history of, C 131; visitations of churches in patronage of (1249–52), C 158(*a*); visitations of churches belonging to (1297, 1458), C 160

St. Petersburg, imports and exports by British factory at (1763), C 169 p. 255

Saint-Sardos, war of (1323–5), C 254

Saints, Pope Alexander III and canonization of, T 68 p. 13

Saints' days, used in dating, G 4 p. 40

Salisbury, city of, Commonwealth charter of (1656), C 180(*d*)

Salisbury, Lord. *See* Cecil, Robert A. T. Gascoyne

SALOMON, FELIX, on foreign policy of Pitt (1784–93), T 20 p. 111

SALTER, FRANK REYNER, on political nonconformity in 1830s, T 76 p. 125

Samson, abbot of Bury St. Edmunds, Kalendar of, C 251

Sandwich, Lord. *See* Montagu, Edward

Sandys, Samuel, memoranda on Parliamentary proceedings by (1722–3), C 261 p. 115

United States of America, history and historians in, T 53 p. 1; proposed treaty with Britain and France on Cuba (1852), T 54 p. 149; emigrant ships to (19th c.), T 55 p. 197; archives of, T 57 p. 55; historiography of, T 69 p. 121, T 77 p. 135; literature on constitutional history of, T 80 p. 159; diplomacy and war plans in (1890–1917), T 84 p. 1; British rivalries with, and emancipation of Spanish America, T 89 p. 131; British rivalries with, in central America, T 91 p. 174; influence of Magna Carta on constitutional development in, M 15 p. 180

Universities, medieval, T 58 p. 1; Englishmen at that of Padua (1460–75), T 60 p. 101; petitions for benefices from English, during papal schism, T 68 p. 41

Uses, statute of, draft, T 60 p. 135

USHER, ROLAND GREENE, *ed.* minute book of Dedham classis (1582–9), C 175

Usury, laws on (18th c.), T 57 p. 197

Vacancies, episcopal, at Ely (1298–9), T 53 p. 49

VALENTIN, VEIT, on Bismarck and England, T 61 p. 13

Valliscaulian order, house of, T 4 p. 1

VAN DER SPRENKEL, O. P. N. B., on China, in *Handbook of oriental history*, G 6 p. 153

VAN WERVEKE, H., on currency manipulation case of Louis de Male, count of Flanders (d. 1384), T 72 p. 115

Varennes, flight of Louis XVI to, T 13 p. 319

VARLEY, FREDERICK JOHN, *ed.* Restoration visitation of Oxford (1660–2), C 246(*c*)

VAUGHAN, RICHARD, *ed.* Chronicle of John of Wallingford, C 257(*a*)

VEITCH, GEORGE STEAD, on Huskisson and Liskeard elections (1802, 1804), T 54 p. 205

Venables, Robert (d. 1687), his narrative of West Indian expedition (1654–5), C 165

Venezuela, Anglo-American rivalries during crisis over (1895), T 90 p. 131; maps of boundaries with British Guiana, T 90 p. 132

Venice, list of ambassadors to England from (1502–1763), C 37 p. vi

VENNING, WILLIAM MARSHALL, on New England Company, T 12 p. 293

Vercingetorix, T 14 p. 1

Vergil, Polydore (d. 1555?), edn. of his *Anglica historia* (1485–1537), C 241; part of English translation of, C 29, C 36; materials for his *History*, T 26 p. 1; note on, T 29 p. 279; will of, T 52 p. 117, p. 131

VERICOUR, LOUIS RAYMOND DE, on study of history, T 1 p. 1; on Jacquerie T 1 p. 187; on medieval Bohemia, T 2 p. 54; on Wat Tyler, T 2 p. 77

VERLINDEN, CHARLES, on Frankish colonization, T 77 p. 1